THE ESSENCE & IMPORTANCE *of* LIVING A PURPOSEFUL *Life*

The man without a purpose is like a ship without a Rudder—a wait, a nothing, a no man.

— Thomas Carlyle

Dr. Linet Ojwang

Copyright © 2025 – The Essence & Importance of Living a Purposeful Life, Linet Ojwang, *all rights reserved.*

All rights reserved. No part of this publication may be reproduced, distributed, or transmitted in any form or by any means, including photocopying, recording, or other electronic or mechanical methods, without the prior written permission of the publisher, except in the case of brief quotations embodied in critical reviews and certain other noncommercial uses permitted by copyright law. For permission requests, write to the publisher, at the address below: ojwanglinet16@gmail.com.

Unless otherwise identified, scripture quotations are taken from the Holy Bible 2025.

Published by: Heavenly Realm Publishing,
www.heavenlyrealmpublishing.com,
1-866-216-0696

Heavenly Realm Publishing
Houston, TX

ISBN 13—9781944383-43-5 (soft cover)
ISBN 13—9781944383-44-2 (hard cover)

1. Religion/ Christian Ministry/ General—United States. 2. Religion/ Christian Ministry/ Counseling & Recovery—United States. 3. Religion/ Christian Ministry/ Evangelism—United States.

This book is available at: Amazon, Barnes & Noble, Books-A-Million, Borders, Walmart, Target and stores near you.

This book is printed on acid free paper.

This book is printed in the USA.

THE ESSENCE & IMPORTANCE *of* LIVING A PURPOSEFUL *Life*

TABLE OF CONTENTS

DEDICATION	7
ACKNOWLEDGEMENT	8
PREFACE	9
CHAPTER ONE: INTRODUCTION	11
• A Brief Look Into Linet Ojwang to Voluntary and Humanitarian Services	11
• Importance of Humanitarian Work in healthcare	19
CHAPTER TWO: EARLY LIFE AND BACKGROUND	29
• Background and Early Influences	29
• Medical and Nursing Education Training	36
• Academic Classes and Nursing Schools	40
• Key Components of Nursing Education	42
• Clinical Training & Hands-On Experience	44
• Specializations in Nursing	45
• Continuous Professional Development	47
• Role of Technology in Nursing Education	49
• Challenges in Nursing Education	51
• Global Perspectives on Nursing Education	52
• Leadership and Healthcare Management	54
• My Medical Leadership and Humanitarian Activities	57
CHAPTER THREE: FINDING ONE PURPOSE	61
• How to Find Your Life Purpose to Live with Intention	64
• Importance of Having a Purpose in Life to Be Happier	65

- Questions That Help You Discover the Purpose of Life — 67
- Understanding the Journey — 70
- Step by Step: How to Answer the Question "What is My Purpose?" — 71
- Identify Values — 72
- Developing Goals and Dream — 78

CHAPTER FOUR: CHALLENGES OF PURPOSEFUL LIVING — 93
- Being a Good Steward of Your Resources — 94
- Being a Good Steward of Our Time — 94
- Being a Good Steward of Our Talents — 98
- Being Good Stewards of Our Treasures — 100
- Being a Good Stewards of The Environment — 103
- Being a Light to Others in The Dark — 105
- Being a Peacemaker in Your Relationship — 108
- Building a Legacy of Faith and Service — 112
- The Power of Gratitude — 115
- The Impact of a Grateful Mindset — 118
- Embracing Challenges as Opportunities for Growth — 119

CHAPTER FIVE: IMPORTANCE OF PURPOSEFUL LIVING — 127
- Importance of Helping Others — 127
- The Role of Purposeful Living in Our Lives — 130
- Cultivating a Spirit of Generosity. — 134
- Embracing your Identity in Christ. — 142
- Encouraging and Uplifting others — 147

CHAPTER SIX: VALUE OF PURPOSEFUL LIVING — 157
- The Value of Being Kind to Others — 157

- The Impact of Excellence ... 164
- The Value of Taking in Strangers ... 168
- Pursuing Meaningful Relationships with God and Others ... 173

CHAPTER SEVEN: SIGNIFICANCE OF PURPOSEFUL LIVING 179
- The Role of Compassion in Purposeful Living ... 180
- The Significance of Feeding the Hungry ... 184
- The Significance of Generosity in Purposeful Living ... 188
- The Significance of Loving in Purposeful Living ... 193
- Love as the Foundation of Purpose ... 193
- The Significance of Serving Others ... 198

CHAPTER EIGHT: IMPACT AND CONTRIBUTION 205
- Impact and Contribution ... 205
- Community Engagement and Education in Kenya ... 206
- Founding Maurice Ojwang Unique Academy ... 206
- Mission Work and Health Fairs ... 207
- Healthcare Leadership and Service in the U.S. ... 207
- Personal and Professional Resilience ... 208
- Core Values and Legacy ... 208

CONCLUSION ... 211
INDEX ... 212
GLOSSARY ... 218
MEET THE AUTHOR ... 224

DEDICATION

This book is dedicated to my late husband Maurice, my partner and greatest supporter, who has been my most profound inspiration for 28 years of marriage.

To my son and daughter, Jr and Princess, who fills my heart with joy daily. To my grandson, AJ (Aaron James) the light of my life.

To my mother and my late father, who never stopped believing in me. They both planted the seed of knowledge in my mind and nurtured it. It always reminded me that words have the power to change the world.

ACKNOWLEDGEMENT

I am extremely thankful for the Bible, which showed me my purpose for life: Matthew 25:42-43. NIV 42. *"For I was hungry, and you gave me nothing to eat, I was thirsty, and you gave me nothing to drink,"* 43. *"I was a stranger, and you did not invite me in, I needed clothes, and you did not clothe me, I was sick and in prison, and you did not look after me."*

I am grateful to the hundreds of writers and teachers, both classical and contemporary, who have shaped my life and helped me learn my purpose in life.

I thank God and you for sharing my experiences and purpose in life with you.

PREFACE

Many of us search for a deeper sense of meaning and purpose in a world that often feels chaotic and overwhelming and has many roles. This book guides that journey, offering practical tools and insights to help you discover your unique calling and live a life filled with passion and purpose.

Whether you're feeling lost, unfulfilled, or simply seeking a greater sense of direction, this book will equip you with the knowledge and inspiration you need to find your path and live a life that truly matters. We'll explore the importance of self-reflection, identifying your values, and setting meaningful goals while fostering hope and resilience.

Prepare to embark on a transformative journey of self-discovery of your purpose in life. After sharing my experiences with others through outreach and mission efforts, I realized I could help others with my life story find their purpose.

In my book, I discuss my experiences and how they changed me. I hope you'll find stories and mementos that will touch your heart. A couple of years I had a tragic event in my life that left me wondering what my purpose is in life. I have had different roles in my lifetime, like a wife, a mother and a worker, but what happens when all these roles are deleted from your life? What becomes your purpose? Exactly 4 years ago, I lost my husband of 28 years in marriage due to COVID-19; I was left unexpectedly with no role of being a wife. Our children have grown, and I am not mothering them like when they were younger; our jobs can end at any time. I was left to wonder, what is my purpose in this life? I pondered and prayed about this issue. It was always on my mind, trying to find my purpose. Several times, I have travelled back home to Kenya in Africa and participated in community health fairs, clothes distribution, and services for underserved communities, and I felt fulfilled. I learnt and volunteered at my local church to serve the homeless population. Here, we serve them hot meals, assist with showers, distribute new clothes, encourage, pray for and with them, read the Bible together and encourage them to move out of the streets and get jobs and other resources. I started discovering that I was getting fulfilled at the end of the day. I was waiting eagerly for the day to come so I could serve the homeless at our local church and community center.

Through all of this, I've realized that my purpose is rooted in service. Helping others and being there for those in need has brought me so much joy and fulfillment. Finally confirmed that, "Service to Humanity Never Expires," by Dr Linet.

PURPOSE 1 LIFE

A Brief Look into Linet Ojwang's Journey in Voluntary and Humanitarian Services.

Linet Ojwang's story is one of profound selflessness, resilience, and a deep commitment to humanitarian service—one that has touched the lives of countless individuals in both her native Kenya and her adopted home in the United States. Her journey into voluntary and humanitarian service reflects not only her personal experiences but also stands as a testament to

Linet's journey is far from over, and her impact continues to grow. Her life serves as an inspiration to anyone seeking to live with purpose.

how one person's unwavering dedication can leave a lasting impact. From early lessons learned from her mother and grandmother to her transformative work in community service, nursing, and mission work, Linet's life embodies compassion, generosity, and purpose.

Linet's exposure to voluntary service began early, deeply rooted in her upbringing. Raised in a devoted Seventh-day Adventist family, she grew up in a household where serving others was a daily practice. Her mother, Dorina Ajwang, was a major influence—consistently modeling empathy, charity, and kindness. Dorena often opened their home to widows and orphans with nowhere else to turn. These early experiences were formative for Linet. She witnessed firsthand how small acts of kindness could transform lives. It was not uncommon to see her mother share food with the less fortunate, even when they had little themselves. This consistent practice of giving without expecting anything in return became a central pillar of Linet's character and shaped her understanding of what it meant to live a life of service.

Even as a young girl, Linet embraced these lessons. While most children her age were preoccupied with play, she found joy in contributing meaningfully to her community. At her local church, Odienya Seventh-day Adventist Church, she became involved in the children's choir—not just as a participant, but as a leader, teaching other children songs and memory verses. Her leadership skills were evident early on, and her passion for music became a channel through which she gave back to her community. For Linet, bringing people together through song was an early form of ministry—her way of offering something beautiful that touched both heart and spirit. Music became one of her first forms of voluntary service, used to uplift others and build unity.

Her commitment to service extended beyond the church. As she grew older, Linet's sense of responsibility grew. During the annual Seventh-day Adventist Week of Prayer, preachers would visit homes to pray for families, often accompanied by children who mimicked their actions. In their small way, they became ministers of hope. Linet recalls one of the most impactful moments from this time: she and her group visited a woman heavily involved in brewing alcohol. Through persistent prayer and visits, this woman eventually abandoned that lifestyle and joined the church. This transformation would not have been possible without Linet and her peers 'quiet faith and determination. The experience cemented Linet's belief in the power of community service and the idea that anyone, regardless of age or status, can make a difference.

Linet's path of service continued into adulthood. After completing her primary and secondary education, she moved to Mombasa for college and began working with the Kenya Ports Authority. Despite the demands of her job, she remained deeply committed to service. Her faith continued to guide her, and she became increasingly involved in her local church, serving as a youth leader. She guided young people in their spiritual journeys, organized church activities, and continued her work in music and preaching. Through her leadership, she mentored youth, helping them navigate adolescence and encouraging them to find purpose through service, as she had.

A major turning point in Linet's life came when she relocated to the United States in the early 1990s after marrying her husband. Moving to a new country brought challenges, but Linet faced them with the same resilience that had defined her journey. In the U.S., her Kenyan qualifications were not immediately recognized, and she had to start over—working first as a nursing assistant while pursuing further education. It was during this time that her calling to serve others grew even stronger. For Linet, nursing was not merely a profession but a vocation. Caring for vulnerable patients aligned deeply with her values. She viewed her work as an extension of her faith—a practical expression of the empathy and service she had learned from a young age.

Linet advanced in her career, becoming a Licensed Practical Nurse (LPN), then a Registered Nurse (RN). She later earned a bachelor's degree in nursing and a Master of Science in Nursing with an emphasis in Leadership in Health Care Systems. As she rose professionally, her ability to serve grew alongside her responsibilities. She managed nursing teams, oversaw patient care, and organized health fairs and outreach programs through her church. Whether at a hospital bedside or in a community setting, Linet remained focused on using her skills to uplift those in need.

In 2009, Linet and her family returned to Kenya for a medical missionary trip held at their former school. Over two days, they served around 400 people each day, including children. Linet enlisted the help of her college-aged children—both biology majors at the time—to assist with taking vital signs, while she handled assessments and triaged severely ill patients to nearby hospitals. However, since Linet was not a medical doctor, she could not diagnose or prescribe medication. Despite this limitation, her work was instrumental in providing critical care and connecting patients with the medical attention they needed. Those two days were incredibly impactful. Linet and her team saw patients until as late as 9 p.m., refusing to leave until everyone had been treated. She remains deeply grateful to her family for the unwavering support they provided during such demanding moments.

That night, as Linet went to bed, her mind was filled with thoughts of how she could better help the people who so desperately needed her. She felt that if she had been a medical doctor, she would have been able to offer even greater assistance. From that moment on, her thoughts were consumed by the idea of going to medical school. She began researching online to explore her options.

After the family returned to the United States, Linet took the MCAT (Medical College Admission Test) and passed. She submitted applications to several medical schools both within the U.S. and abroad. While she received responses from multiple institutions, none offered scholarships. Then, one Sabbath afternoon after a full day at church, Linet came home to find a letter from the University of Health Sciences Antigua. To her surprise, the letter stated that the university offered full benefits to those already in the medical field—including nurses. Linet could hardly believe it. Her husband quickly verified the information, and it was true.

Linet enrolled in the university in September 2009 and graduated in 2014 with a Doctor of Medicine (M.D.) degree. Upon returning to the U.S., she faced new challenges. Her family needed funds to send their two children to college, and due to the high cost of living, she had to return to work to support her husband, who had been the sole provider during her five years in medical school.

Linet took on the responsibility of helping cover her children's college expenses, completing the construction of their school back in Kenya, supporting extended families, and continuing to meet her financial obligations in the U.S.

One of the most impactful ways Linet and her husband gave back to the community was through the founding of Maurice Ojwang Unique Academy in Kenya. This school was established to educate children who could not afford school fees. For Linet, education was not merely a tool for academic success—it was a powerful means of empowerment and community transformation. The school offered early education to children from underprivileged backgrounds. Linet and her husband sponsored many of these students, ensuring they had access to the same quality education she herself had been fortunate to receive. The impact of this school is immeasurable; it has provided countless children with the foundation they need to pursue further education and build better futures.

Beyond education, Linet's humanitarian efforts extended to mission work—particularly in Kenya. In 1998, she and her husband organized a mission trip that brought around 30 individuals from their U.S. church to Kenya. The experience was life-changing for all involved. The group provided healthcare services, distributed clothing, and offered counseling and community support. For Linet, this mission work was a natural extension of her lifelong desire to serve. It created a bridge between her life in the United States and her roots in Kenya, bringing much-needed resources to underserved communities. The group also sponsored additional students at their academy.

Linet's dedication to service has remained unwavering, even in the face of personal tragedy. In 2020, her husband passed away from COVID-19—a devastating loss of her life partner and collaborator in service. Despite her grief, Linet stayed committed to her calling. She relocated to be closer to her children and entered a period of deep reflection. During this time, she realized her purpose had always been to serve others, and that realization gave her the strength to continue. She believes that God spared her life during the pandemic for a reason. In contrast to the many lives lost, her survival deepened her sense of responsibility to carry on the humanitarian work they had begun together.

Today, Linet's story is one of resilience, faith, and enduring service. She continues to serve as a healthcare leader, but her true focus remains on using her skills and experience to uplift others—especially the underserved. Whether through her work in healthcare, her involvement in church, or her continued support for the Maurice Ojwang Unique Academy, Linet's life is a testament to the power of service. She has found that true fulfillment comes not from personal achievement or material gain, but from making a meaningful difference in the lives of others.

Linet's journey is far from over, and her impact continues to grow. Her life serves as an inspiration to anyone seeking to live with purpose. She reminds us that there is always an opportunity to serve—especially in the face of hardship. For Linet, service is not just something she does—it is who she is. Her story reminds us that when we dedicate ourselves to helping others, we not only improve the lives around us but also discover our own true purpose in the process.

The Importance of Humanitarian Work in Health Care

Humanitarian work in nursing is essential for addressing health disparities, promoting public health, and delivering care where medical services are scarce or inaccessible. For nurses, engaging in humanitarian efforts expands the scope of their profession beyond traditional clinical settings. It allows them to apply their expertise in crisis zones, underserved communities, and regions affected by natural disasters, conflict, or widespread poverty. These efforts reach populations that are often overlooked or forgotten, offering critical care and hope. Humanitarian health work also fosters a deeper understanding of global health issues, enhances cultural competence, and sharpens adaptability—as nurses often work with limited resources in unpredictable environments.

Providing Care to Vulnerable Populations

Humanitarian nursing is vital because it brings life-saving care to regions where healthcare is either limited or completely unavailable. In crises—such as natural disasters, armed conflict, or extreme poverty—local medical infrastructure is often overwhelmed or nonexistent. In these situations, nurses are often among the first responders, managing everything from routine ailments to acute, life-threatening conditions.

Their responsibilities are broad and include immunizations, maternal and child health services, wound care, and chronic disease management. This is especially important in areas where diseases like malaria, tuberculosis, and HIV are prevalent. By providing these essential services, humanitarian nurses not only save lives but also bring dignity, stability, and healing to some of the world's most vulnerable populations.

Often, the only thing standing between life and death is the steady, compassionate presence of a nurse willing to serve in the shadows.

Promoting Public Health

Beyond immediate care, humanitarian healthcare workers play a pivotal role in improving long-term public health. In communities where people live in crowded, unsanitary conditions—such as refugee camps—nurses are on the frontlines preventing the spread of disease. Their work involves education around hygiene, sanitation, and basic health practices: how to wash hands properly, access safe drinking water, and dispose of waste—all crucial steps in preventing outbreaks of diseases like cholera, dysentery, or COVID-19.

These educational efforts may seem simple, but their impact is transformative. They empower communities to care for themselves, reduce dependency, and create sustainable health solutions. In doing so, nurses don't just treat symptoms—they build the foundation for healthier futures.

Upholding Nursing Values of Compassion and Care

Compassion, empathy, and dignity lie at the heart of nursing—and humanitarian work exemplifies these values at their highest level.

In this field, nurses care for people who have lost everything: their homes, loved ones, and sense of safety. These individuals are not only in need of medical care but are often coping with psychological trauma and the emotional weight of survival.

Humanitarian nurses provide more than physical treatment. They offer comfort, presence, and reassurance in times of profound distress. They listen, hold hands, wipe tears, and sit silently with patients who have no words left. In doing so, they restore a sense of humanity where it has been torn away. In crises, where fear is loud and hope is fragile, nurses become beacons of compassion and stability.

Developing Critical Professional Skills

Working in humanitarian settings demands resilience, creativity, and quick decision-making. Nurses often provide care with minimal equipment, limited medication, and no reliable power or water. They must improvise, innovate and adapt constantly—finding new ways to sterilize tools, deliver treatments, or triage emergencies.

This kind of work refines leadership, critical thinking, and crisis management skills. Nurses who engage in humanitarian missions often return to their regular duties more capable, more confident, and more inspired. Their experiences sharpen their professional edge while deepening their sense of purpose. They don't just learn how to work under pressure—they learn how to lead under it.

Enhancing Cultural Competence

Humanitarian nursing offers a powerful opportunity to engage with people from diverse cultural backgrounds. Nurses working abroad must often navigate different languages, customs, and healthcare beliefs. Whether serving in rural Africa, Southeast Asia, or the Middle East, they must listen deeply, observe respectfully, and respond sensitively.

These encounters help nurses develop cultural competence—an essential skill for providing patient-centered care. Understanding and honoring local traditions can improve patient outcomes and build lasting trust. For example, a nurse who respects traditional healing practices while offering modern treatment can create a bridge between two worlds, fostering healing that respects both science and culture.

As our world becomes more connected, this ability to work across cultures is not just valuable—it's essential.

Offering a Sense of Purpose and Fulfillment

While all nursing can be meaningful, humanitarian nursing often brings an especially profound sense of purpose. Whether helping deliver a baby in a refugee camp or comforting a patient in the aftermath of disaster, humanitarian nurses witness the immediate, life-changing impact of their efforts.

This work connects nurses to something larger than themselves. It renews their spirit, deepens their sense of vocation, and often becomes a defining chapter of their careers. Many return home changed—not just professionally, but personally. They carry with them not just stories, but a deeper understanding of resilience, gratitude, and the power of kindness.

In the quiet moments after chaos, in the grateful smiles of those they serve, humanitarian nurses find something rare and priceless: a sense that their work truly matters.

Building Global Healthcare Capacity

One of the most transformative aspects of humanitarian nursing is its role in strengthening healthcare capacity in underserved regions. Humanitarian nurses often collaborate with local healthcare providers, sharing knowledge, training, and skills that build and reinforce the local healthcare system. This may include teaching local nurses, midwives, and community health workers or advocating for improved clinical practices.

By empowering local practitioners, humanitarian nurses help establish sustainable systems of care that endure long after the mission has ended. This kind of capacity-building is especially vital in communities with limited infrastructure and a shortage of skilled professionals. Through their presence, humanitarian nurses don't just bring temporary relief—they leave behind the tools and training that enable communities to care for their own. In doing so, they light a spark of self-reliance and dignity, offering something more lasting than medicine alone: hope for a healthier future.

Improving Global Health Equity

A central mission of humanitarian nursing is to challenge and eliminate health inequities while advancing global health equity. In many parts of the world, healthcare is a privilege—not a guaranteed right. Millions are denied access to even the most basic medical services simply because of where they live, their socioeconomic status, or ongoing political unrest.

Humanitarian nurses step into these neglected corners of the world with the goal of changing that reality. By offering their expertise in places often overlooked, they help level the playing field and restore dignity to those who have been left behind. This is especially vital in tackling issues like maternal and infant mortality, infectious diseases, and malnutrition—problems that disproportionately affect impoverished communities.

Ultimately, humanitarian nursing is not just about treating patients—it's about advocating for a world in which every human being, regardless of circumstance, has access to care, comfort, and a chance to live. In their service, humanitarian nurses become voices for justice, healing agents of equity, and champions for the right to health.

Contributing to Personal and Professional Growth

Humanitarian work pushes nurses far beyond their comfort zones, fostering both professional excellence and personal transformation. Working in unfamiliar environments, managing limited resources, and making quick, life-saving decisions in high-pressure situations demands resilience, innovation, and courage. These experiences cultivate a deeper understanding of healthcare and refine essential skills like leadership, adaptability and cultural competence. However, beyond the clinical growth lies something more profound: a changed perspective on life itself. Humanitarian nurses often return home with a renewed sense of gratitude, humility and empathy. They carry the stories of those they served—stories of suffering, strength, survival that allow those stories to shape who they are as healers and as people.

In the eyes of a mother whose child was saved, in the smile of a patient recovering in a makeshift clinic, nurses rediscover why they chose this calling in the first place. The impact is not only outward—it echoes inward, enriching their lives with deeper meaning and lasting purpose.

Responding to Global Crises

In times of global crisis—pandemics, natural disasters, armed conflict—humanitarian nurses are among the first to respond and the last to leave. These events often stretch local healthcare systems to the breaking point, leaving communities vulnerable and underserved.

Humanitarian nurses stand in the gap. They provide emergency care, contain disease outbreaks, and support overstretched healthcare infrastructures. Their ability to act swiftly and effectively is crucial to reducing the human toll of such crises. During the COVID-19 pandemic, for example, the world witnessed the power of a global nursing network—professionals who stepped forward in unprecedented numbers, often at great personal risk, to care for strangers in need.

These nurses are more than caregivers; they are protectors of hope in humanity's darkest hours. Their presence says, "You are not forgotten. You matter." They bring stability in chaos, healing in fear, and the reassurance that even amid the worst of times, compassion has not left the world.

EARLY LIFE 2 AND BACKGROUND

Background and Early Influences.

My life journey began in a small village in Kenya, where I was born the youngest of four children. Growing up in a close-knit family, I was always surrounded by love, but I also learned the importance of responsibility from an early age. Being the last-born didn't mean I was carefree or spoiled. Instead, I felt drawn to the values my parents instilled in us: hard work, community, and a deep sense of caring for others.

My father, Johnson Ayieko Okundi, worked in Nairobi, while my mother, Dorena Ajwang, stayed home to care for the family. My childhood was shaped by the rhythm of my father's travels between the city and our rural home, and we would often journey to Nairobi to visit him. Though he wasn't always physically present, his influence and wisdom were constant. Meanwhile, my mother provided the daily care, warmth, and spiritual foundation that made our home full of life and love. It was a busy household but always filled with a strong sense of togetherness. I learned early that family was everything.

As a child, I witnessed my mother's boundless generosity. Our home was never just for us—it became a refuge for widows, orphans, and anyone in need. She shared what little we had without hesitation, teaching me that true kindness isn't measured by abundance, but by a willingness to give. My siblings and I would often help deliver food to struggling families or spend time with those who felt alone. These moments planted the seed of purpose in my heart—a quiet realization that life's greatest meaning is found in serving others.

Faith was another cornerstone of our lives. As a Seventh-day Adventist family, attending church every Sabbath wasn't just a routine—it was a cherished part of our identity. At Odienya Seventh-day Adventist Church, I discovered a love for music, reading, and the powerful stories of the Bible. I joined the children's choir, the Sabbath class and soon began leading songs and helping teach memory verses. Even at that young age, guiding others gave me a deep sense of fulfillment—a small glimpse into the calling that would one day shape my life's work.

Education was a high priority in our home, especially for my father. He believed it was the key to a brighter future and worked tirelessly to ensure all of us had the opportunity to go to school. I began my studies at Primary School and took my education seriously, knowing what it meant to my family. At the same time, I remained deeply involved in our daily responsibilities at home. After school, my siblings and I would tend to the family's livestock—cows, goats, and sheep—tasks that taught us patience, consistency, and humility. It was a life of balance, blending academic focus with hands-on responsibility, and it laid the foundation for my work ethic.

At church, I joined the baptismal class, where we learned memory verses, Bible stories, and how to apply spiritual principles to our young lives. The class lasted a full year, culminating in a baptism during the annual Seventh-day Adventist camp meeting—a vibrant event where churches from various areas came together. We'd gather for worship, music, preaching, and fellowship. One memory stands out clearly: the rare and much-loved peanut butter soup, made only once a year during the harvest season. For us children, that dish was symbolic—of celebration, of unity, and of something truly special.

That particular year, I was set to be baptized. My siblings had all gone ahead to the camp meeting, but I was left behind to care for the livestock. Still, my determination didn't waver. I knew where the baptism was happening—at nearby river on Friday of camp meeting week. I took the animals to graze near the river, then joined the baptism candidates in my everyday clothes. As others lined up in white garments, I stood among them in my home clothes and stepped into the water. I was baptized and then returned to tend the animals. On Sabbath, I rejoined the community for worship and was officially welcomed with the other newly baptized members.

My parents were so proud—not just because I was baptized, but because I made that decision independently. I learned that day that accepting Jesus as your personal Savior is, indeed, a personal choice that no one can make for you.

When it was time to transition to secondary school, my life took a significant turn. I moved to Nairobi to live with my eldest sister so I could attend High School. The move to the city was a major shift from the serenity of village life. Nairobi was fast-paced, noisy, and full of opportunity—but it also presented new challenges. I had to adapt quickly, but I carried the values I'd learned at home like humility, faith, respect and perseverance.

The transition wasn't always easy, but it broadened my perspective and opened doors I never imagined possible. It allowed me to dream beyond the boundaries of my village and planted the early seeds of what would become a lifelong journey of purpose, compassion, and service.

After a few years in Nairobi, I moved once more—this time to Mombasa—where my uncle believed I would benefit from the structure and discipline of boarding school. I enrolled at a High School, where I completed my secondary education. Boarding school was yet another adjustment, but it gave me something invaluable: independence. I learned to manage my time and responsibilities without the daily support of my family. It was both challenging and empowering.

Through all these transitions, one thing remained constant—my faith. Every Sabbath, a group of Seventh-day Adventist students from my school was allowed to worship at a nearby local church. These weekly gatherings became a spiritual anchor for me. It was during this time that my leadership skills began to bloom further. I continued to sing, to organize youth participation, and I even started preaching in those local churches. These small but powerful moments of service deepened my love for ministry and helped me find my voice—literally and figuratively.

The annual Seventh-day Adventist camp meetings also remained a highlight of my spiritual life. These large gatherings brought together churches from across the region. The music, the fellowship, and the powerful sermons reminded me that faith and community are inseparable. They reinforced my calling: to serve, to lead, and to give.

My childhood, however, wasn't without its hardships. Growing up in a rural village meant resources were often limited, and we had to work hard for everything we had. But those challenges taught me resilience. One of my earliest responsibilities was helping care for our livestock after school—cows, goats, and sheep. It was tiring work, but it gave me purpose. I wasn't just a child; I was a contributor to my family's well-being. That sense of responsibility planted the seeds of maturity early on.

Among the most formative influences in my life was my father. Though often away in Nairobi for work, he placed a deep trust in me, even at a young age. I still remember how, at just seven or eight years old, he would leave me with the family finances during his trips. Together, we would plan how to use the money—for school fees, food, or household needs. It was a great responsibility for a child, but he trusted me, and that trust shaped me. It taught me accountability, financial wisdom, and the importance of stewarding resources for the greater good.

My father wasn't just practical—he was visionary. He believed wholeheartedly in the power of education, and he was determined that all his children, including me, would have the chance to learn and succeed, regardless of the obstacles. This was especially meaningful in a community where many girls did not have that opportunity. His belief in me became a source of strength that I carried into every stage of my life.

Looking back now, I see how profoundly those early years shaped who I am. My parents, my faith, and my village community all contributed to the foundation of my character. Whether I was tending to animals, managing household finances, learning Bible verses, or leading the children's choir, each experience instilled in me values that have lasted a lifetime: service, integrity, humility, and perseverance.

As I grew into adulthood, these lessons never left me. My mother's boundless compassion, my father's unwavering commitment to education, and the powerful sense of belonging that came from our church and village—they all became threads woven into the fabric of my life. Whether in my work in healthcare, my role in the church, or my humanitarian outreach, I have always strived to live out those values.

My early life laid the foundation for everything that followed. The lessons I learned about responsibility, resilience, and service continue to guide me through both challenges and opportunities. Even today, I often reflect on the simplicity and strength of those village days. The roots of my story lie in that small corner of Kenya, but their reach has grown far beyond. The impact of those early years echoes not only in my life but in the lives of those I've been blessed to serve.

And that, to me, is the truest measure of a life well lived—not how far you've gone, but how many you've helped along the way.

Medical and Nursing Education Training

Medical and nursing education and training are the cornerstones of any effective healthcare system. They ensure that healthcare professionals are equipped with the knowledge, skills, and ethical grounding necessary to provide safe, competent and compassionate care. Nurses, often regarded as the backbone of healthcare, have seen their roles evolve significantly—demanding a stronger educational foundation than ever before. Becoming a nurse today requires rigorous academic training combined with hands-on clinical experience—both essential for navigating the complexities of modern healthcare environments. The level of education pursued—whether diploma, associate, bachelor's, or advanced degree—defines the depth of training and the career opportunities available. Still, at every level, a solid educational framework is non-negotiable.

Having obtained my Master of Science in Nursing and served in several leadership roles within the healthcare system, I found myself yearning for deeper knowledge—particularly in medicine and healthcare policy. This drive led me to pursue a Doctor of Medicine (M.D.), which I proudly completed in 2014. This achievement allowed me to merge my nursing foundation with advanced medical knowledge, significantly enhancing my ability to lead in hospital and community-based healthcare settings.

Medical school was demanding—emotionally, intellectually, and physically. The intensity of coursework and clinical rotations stretched my abilities but also widened my perspective on patient care. It gave me firsthand insight into the challenges of clinical medicine and reinforced the importance of interdisciplinary collaboration in delivering effective, holistic care.

Medical school presents a variety of challenges that require careful navigation. Some of them include demanding workload and its impact on mental health, as well as the importance of effective time management and work-life balance.

The intense curriculum necessitates the absorption of a vast amount of information at a rapid pace, which can be overwhelming. It is crucial to acknowledge the stress associated with high-stakes exams and evaluations, as this pressure can lead to significant anxiety.

Additionally, balancing coursework, studying, clinical rotations, and extracurricular activities require strong time management skills. I believe it is important to share strategies that can help us manage these demands effectively.

Financial considerations also play a significant role in the medical school experience. The high tuition costs can lead to substantial student loan debt, and I feel fortunate to have received scholarships that alleviate some of this burden. However, the cost of living in areas near medical schools can be quite high while adding to the financial strain. The intense demands of medical school can lead to burnout, which often manifests as emotional exhaustion, cynicism, and a noticeable decline in performance. I think it's crucial for us to recognize the signs of burnout early and explore strategies to manage our workload effectively.

Additionally, the pressure to excel academically and clinically can result in elevated levels of stress and anxiety. It's important that environment is created where students can share their experiences and support one another in coping with these pressures.

Mental health is another significant concern, as medical students are at a higher risk for issues such as depression, anxiety, and substance abuse. I believe we should foster a culture that prioritizes mental well-being and encourages seeking help when needed.

Balancing the rigorous demands of our studies with personal life can be quite challenging, often leading to feelings of isolation and a lack of work.

My desire to lead meaningful change, influence healthcare policies and advocate for patient-centered reform fueled my pursuit of the M.D. Today, my dual background as a nurse and physician allows me to approach healthcare challenges from a unique, integrative perspective. I've focused my leadership on creating collaborative, team-based environments where the patient's well-being remains the central priority.

Throughout my journey, I have led healthcare teams, driven quality improvement initiatives, and contributed to improved patient outcomes. By combining the empathetic approach of nursing with the analytical depth of medicine, I've been able to bridge care gaps, empower teams, and advance a model of healthcare that is both compassionate and evidence-driven.

Academic Classes and Nursing Schools

The path to becoming a nurse is diverse and offers multiple academic routes tailored to various professional goals. These include diploma programs, associate degrees, bachelor's degrees, and graduate-level degrees, each with its own scope, rigor, and opportunities.

Once the most common entry point into nursing, diploma

programs—typically hospital-based—now play a reduced role in many countries. These programs provide intensive, skills-focused education but are gradually being replaced by academic degree tracks that offer broader knowledge and flexibility.

The Associate Degree in Nursing (ADN) remains a popular two- to three-year program, especially in the U.S., often offered through community colleges. It prepares students for licensure as Registered Nurses (RNs) and equips them with essential clinical competencies. ADN programs are cost-effective and provide a quicker route into the profession, appealing to those with financial or time constraints. However, as healthcare becomes more complex, there is increasing emphasis on higher education for nurses.

The Bachelor of Science in Nursing (BSN) has emerged as the preferred qualification for RNs in many countries. This four-year degree provides a more comprehensive education that includes not only clinical skills but also training in leadership, healthcare policy, research methodology, and public health. BSN-prepared nurses are better positioned for career advancement and are often favored for supervisory and specialized roles.

For those seeking to specialize or step into advanced practice, the next logical progression is the Master of Science in Nursing (MSN) or the Doctor of Nursing Practice (DNP). The MSN prepares nurses for roles such as nurse practitioners, nurse anesthetists, or clinical nurse specialists, combining clinical training with advanced coursework in pathophysiology, diagnostics, and pharmacology. These roles demand independent decision-making and are pivotal in expanding access to care.

The DNP represents the highest level of clinical nursing education and focuses on system-level leadership, policy influence, and clinical excellence. DNP graduates often lead large-scale quality improvement initiatives, conduct implementation research, or serve in executive positions shaping the future of healthcare delivery.

Key Components of Nursing Education

A strong nursing curriculum must integrate both theoretical and practical training. Core subjects include anatomy, physiology, microbiology, pharmacology, and pathophysiology. These disciplines form the scientific foundation of nursing and are essential for understanding how the body functions, how diseases progress, and how medications interact with biological systems. Anatomy and physiology provide essential insights into the structure and function of the human body, enabling nurses to accurately assess patients and deliver effective care.

Microbiology helps students understand the role of pathogens and the importance of infection prevention—a critical skill in all healthcare settings.

Pharmacology gives nurses the tools to administer medications safely, monitor for side effects, and educate patients about their treatments.

Pathophysiology deepens the understanding of disease mechanisms and equips nurses to anticipate clinical deterioration and act swiftly.

Equally vital are courses in ethics, communication, and holistic patient care. Nurses often find themselves at the intersection of critical decision-making and vulnerable moments in a patient's life. Ethical training ensures that they uphold patient autonomy, confidentiality, and dignity, even in complex situations.

Communication skills are heavily emphasized, as nurses must engage with patients, families, and interdisciplinary teams. Whether explaining procedures, delivering difficult news, or collaborating on care plans, effective communication is essential to safe and compassionate care.

Patient care courses focus on health assessment, care planning, and critical thinking. Students learn to conduct thorough patient evaluations, design personalized care plans, and adapt interventions based on changing clinical conditions. These courses reinforce the patient-centered philosophy that defines modern nursing.

Nursing is not just a profession—it is a calling. One that demands not only intellect and skill but also heart and humanity. As someone who has walked the path from rural Kenya to advanced medical and nursing degrees, I have come to believe deeply that education is the most powerful catalyst for transforming individuals, communities, and entire healthcare systems.

The integration of medical and nursing training has empowered me to see the patient not just through the lens of disease but through the lens of dignity, empathy, and possibility. It is this holistic perspective that I carry forward in every role I assume—whether as a caregiver, a leader, or an advocate.

Because in the end, healthcare is not just about treating illness. It's about healing people.

Clinical Training & Hands-On Experience

One of the most essential components of nursing education is clinical training, where students gain hands-on experience in real-world healthcare settings. Clinical rotations are a cornerstone of every nursing curriculum, allowing students to apply theoretical knowledge in practical environments. These rotations typically take place in hospitals, long-term care facilities, clinics, and community health centers, giving students exposure to the many facets of nursing care.

During clinical rotations, nursing students work under the supervision of experienced nurses and clinical instructors. They learn to perform various tasks, including administering medications, monitoring vital signs, providing wound care, and assisting in surgeries or childbirth. Clinical training also develops vital soft skills such as communication, teamwork, adaptability, and time management—skills that are indispensable in fast-paced healthcare environments. One of the most critical outcomes of clinical practice is the ability to remain calm and focused under pressure while maintaining patient safety as the highest priority. In addition, clinical rotations expose students to multiple nursing specialties such as pediatrics, geriatrics, mental health, and critical care. This exposure is pivotal in helping students identify areas of interest and align their future careers with their strengths and passions. For many, clinical training is not just about acquiring skills—it's about building the confidence and professional identity required to transition into a successful nursing career.

Specializations in Nursing

One of the greatest strengths of the nursing profession is the wide range of specializations available. Specializing allows nurses to deepen their knowledge and provide targeted, high-quality care to specific patient populations. Among the most common nursing specialties are pediatric nursing, mental health nursing, critical care nursing, and geriatric nursing.

Pediatric nursing focuses on caring for newborns, children, and adolescents. Pediatric nurses are trained to understand the unique physiological and emotional needs of young patients. They work closely with families and play a key role in delivering everything from routine check-ups and vaccinations to the management of chronic and acute conditions.

Mental health nursing addresses the growing demand for healthcare professionals who can compassionately care for individuals experiencing mental health challenges. Mental health nurses assess, diagnose, and treat conditions such as depression, anxiety, schizophrenia, and bipolar disorder. They work collaboratively with psychiatrists, psychologists, and social workers to deliver holistic, patient-centered care.

Critical care nursing, also known as intensive care nursing, involves the care of critically ill or injured patients. These nurses work in high-acuity environments such as ICUs, where they monitor unstable patients, administer complex treatments, and make rapid decisions that can be lifesaving. The knowledge and precision required in critical care nursing are extensive, reflecting the complexity of the patients they serve.

Geriatric nursing is increasingly important as global populations age. Geriatric nurses specialize in addressing the multifaceted needs of older adults, many of whom manage multiple chronic conditions. These nurses play a vital role in helping seniors maintain independence and quality of life, whether in home care, assisted living, or long-term care facilities.

Beyond these areas, nurses can pursue advanced practice roles such as nurse practitioners, nurse midwives, and nurse anesthetists. These roles require graduate-level education but offer greater autonomy and expanded responsibilities in diagnosis, treatment, and prescribing. For example, nurse practitioners can often manage patient care independently or in collaboration with physicians.

Nursing specialization not only enhances career opportunities but also elevates the quality of patient care by allowing nurses to bring focused expertise to the populations they serve.

Continuous Professional Development

In today's fast-evolving healthcare landscape, continuous professional development (CPD) is essential. With medical knowledge, technology, and treatment protocols constantly advancing, nurses must remain lifelong learners to provide safe and effective care.

CPD includes a broad range of educational activities—formal coursework, workshops, conferences, online learning, and certification programs. These learning opportunities help nurses stay current, expand their competencies, and adopt evidence-based practices.

Obtaining professional certifications in specialized areas is a significant part of career advancement for many nurses. Certifications demonstrate a nurse's proficiency in a specific field and often lead to increased responsibilities and leadership roles. Examples include:

- CCRN for critical care,
- CPN for pediatrics,
- certifications in wound care, diabetes management, and more.

These credentials typically require passing a rigorous examination and maintaining continued education to stay certified.

In addition to formal certifications, many nurses participate in continuing education courses that address emerging topics such as pain management, infection control, palliative care, and digital health tools. These courses are offered by universities, professional organizations, and healthcare institutions, and in many countries, continuing education is a requirement for license renewal.

CPD is also critical for nurses aspiring to leadership and management roles. Training in healthcare policy, team dynamics, budgeting, and conflict resolution equips nurses to take on administrative responsibilities and shape the strategic direction of care delivery. Strong leadership in nursing not only improves workflow and morale but also enhances patient safety and organizational performance.

Role of Technology in Nursing Education

Technology has revolutionized nursing education in recent years, introducing innovative tools that significantly enhance both learning and clinical training. One of the most transformative advancements is the use of simulation labs, where students can practice essential clinical skills in a controlled, safe environment. These labs are equipped with high-fidelity mannequins capable of simulating real-life scenarios—such as childbirth, cardiac arrest, or respiratory failure—offering students realistic experiences without putting actual patients at risk.

Simulation-based training allows students to perform procedures like IV insertion, medication administration, wound care, and CPR with confidence. More importantly, it fosters the development of critical decision-making, clinical judgment, and communication skills in high-stakes scenarios. For example, students may be placed in a virtual emergency room where they must assess patient conditions, prioritize interventions, and coordinate with other healthcare professionals—experiences that are invaluable in preparing them for the demands of real-world practice.

E-learning is another technological innovation that has redefined accessibility in nursing education. Online courses and digital platforms now allow students to pursue degrees while balancing work and family responsibilities. Through these platforms, learners can access lecture materials, participate in discussions, and submit assignments remotely, offering flexibility and inclusivity for diverse student populations.

In addition to simulations and e-learning, mobile apps, online databases, and interactive tools have become indispensable in helping nursing students absorb and retain information. Digital resources such as flashcards, case studies, and medical calculators allow for on-the-go learning, while adaptive quizzes help students track their progress and identify areas for improvement.

Together, these technologies are not only reshaping how nursing is taught—they are also empowering a new generation of nurses to enter the workforce more competent, confident, and technologically literate than ever before.

Challenges in Nursing Education

While nursing education plays a crucial role in preparing skilled healthcare professionals, it also presents significant challenges. One of the most common is the academic intensity of nursing programs. Students often juggle demanding coursework, clinical hours, and personal responsibilities, leading to stress and, in some cases, burnout. For those who work part-time or care for families, this balancing act can be particularly overwhelming.

Financial burdens also remain a major obstacle. While diploma and associate degree programs may be more affordable, pursuing a Bachelor of Science in Nursing (BSN) or an advanced degree often requires substantial financial investment. Tuition, books, uniforms, transportation, and clinical supplies can place a heavy strain on students. While scholarships, grants, and student loan programs offer relief, many aspiring nurses still find the cost of education a barrier to entry or advancement.

For educators, maintaining the balance between theory and practice is another critical challenge. While classroom instruction is foundational, students must also gain sufficient clinical exposure to develop confidence and competency. In many regions, shortages of clinical placements or qualified instructors make it difficult to provide hands-on learning opportunities. In high-demand specialties such as critical care, pediatrics, or mental health, placements may be limited, further complicating efforts to provide well-rounded training.

Additionally, keeping nursing curricula up to date is an ongoing challenge in a constantly evolving healthcare landscape. Advances in medical technology, evolving treatment protocols, and new healthcare policies require educators to continuously revise content and integrate current best practices. This demands close collaboration between academic institutions, healthcare systems, and regulatory bodies to ensure nursing education remains relevant, responsive, and future-ready.

Global Perspectives on Nursing Education

Nursing education varies widely across the globe, shaped by each country's healthcare system, cultural values, and educational infrastructure. In some nations, such as the United States and Canada, nursing programs are highly standardized and regulated by national boards, which set curriculum requirements, licensure criteria, and clinical hour mandates. These systems ensure consistency in graduate competency and readiness for professional licensure exams.

In contrast, other countries—particularly low- and middle-income nations—may have less formalized nursing education systems. Programs may be shorter, focus heavily on basic skills, and be limited in resources. Yet there is growing recognition of the need to strengthen nursing education in these regions to address the global shortage of trained healthcare providers.

International organizations such as the World Health Organization (WHO) and the International Council of Nurses (ICN) play a vital role in promoting global standards, developing training resources, and encouraging knowledge exchange. Their efforts are essential in advancing a global nursing workforce capable of responding to international health challenges.

The scope of nursing practice also differs greatly across borders. In countries like the U.S. and Canada, nurse practitioners are granted significant autonomy and can independently diagnose, prescribe, and manage patient care. Conversely, in many other parts of the world, nurses function primarily under physician oversight, with limited decision-making authority. Despite these differences, the global trend is moving toward professionalizing nursing and expanding educational pathways to include advanced practice roles such as clinical nurse specialists, nurse midwives, and nurse educators.

Many nations are also transitioning toward requiring a BSN as the minimum qualification for entry-level nursing positions—a sign of the growing appreciation for the complexity of modern nursing roles. This shift reflects a broader understanding of the critical role nurses play in achieving global health equity, improving outcomes, and sustaining healthcare systems worldwide.

The integration of technology, the rising importance of specialization, and the global evolution of nursing education all point to one undeniable truth: nurses are not just caregivers—they are leaders, innovators, and advocates. The future of healthcare depends on their ability to adapt, learn, and lead in an ever-changing world.

Leadership and Healthcare Management

In my current role as a healthcare leader, I am responsible for overseeing the efficient operation of hospital departments, maintaining high standards of patient care, and leading teams of healthcare professionals dedicated to improving health outcomes. This responsibility extends beyond day-to-day management—it involves aligning our hospital's strategic goals with the evolving needs of the community and the broader healthcare landscape.

The complexity of my work requires a comprehensive understanding of healthcare systems, the ability to anticipate challenges, and the foresight to implement solutions that meet both present and future objectives. It is a dynamic environment that demands agility, vision, and unwavering dedication.

Teamwork plays a central role in my leadership philosophy. Healthcare is inherently multidisciplinary, and fostering a collaborative environment is essential. Every team member—whether a doctor, nurse, administrator, or support staff—has a vital role to play in achieving our shared goal: delivering the best possible care to our patients. I believe that success is built on effective communication, mutual respect, and the ability to listen and learn from one another. By encouraging open dialogue and the exchange of ideas, I've cultivated a workplace culture where innovation and collaboration thrive.

Empathy is equally vital in leadership. Healthcare decisions often affect not only systems but also individual lives. I strive to lead with compassion, always considering the human impact of every decision—on patients, staff, and the community. This empathetic approach fosters resilience during challenging times and ensures that patients feel seen, heard, and valued, regardless of their background or condition. It also supports the mental, emotional, and physical well-being of the caregivers who serve them.

As a healthcare executive, I am deeply committed to data-driven decision-making. In today's complex healthcare environment, using accurate, real-time data is essential for improving patient outcomes and operational performance. I leverage data to identify trends, monitor key performance indicators, and adapt strategies accordingly. Whether it's integrating new technologies, optimizing resource allocation, or streamlining clinical workflows, informed decisions enable our organization to stay ahead of emerging challenges and deliver consistently high-quality care.

One of the enduring challenges of healthcare leadership is finding the right balance between clinical insight and organizational management. My experience has taught me that effective leadership is not just about managing processes—it's about creating an environment in which healthcare workers can thrive. This means providing access to professional development, ensuring resources are available to meet clinical needs, and supporting policies that promote a healthy work-life balance. A well-supported and motivated team is the foundation of exceptional patient care.

Leadership also requires making tough decisions—particularly in resource-constrained situations or during times of crisis. I have learned that such decisions must always be grounded in ethics, purpose, and compassion. Whether facing staffing shortages, public health emergencies, or regulatory changes, I remain focused on maintaining the integrity of care while keeping the team unified and mission-driven.

Ultimately, leadership in healthcare is not about maintaining authority—it's about empowering others. It's about building systems where healthcare professionals feel supported, patients feel genuinely cared for, and every individual is working together toward a common vision: health, healing, and compassionate care.

My Medical Leadership and Humanitarian Activities

My background in both nursing and medicine has given me a unique and powerful perspective—one that allows me to extend my impact beyond individual patient care to address broader public health challenges, particularly among underserved populations. Throughout my career, I have remained deeply committed to merging medical expertise with leadership and humanitarian service, both locally and internationally. This fusion enables me to not only meet immediate clinical needs but also to design and implement sustainable, long-term strategies that improve community health outcomes in areas facing significant barriers to care.

Whether leading healthcare initiatives in disadvantaged communities or championing our hospital's outreach programs, my approach is consistently driven by a desire to leverage available resources, knowledge, and partnerships to uplift those most in need. In these roles, I have witnessed firsthand how access to quality healthcare can transform lives. These experiences continue to fuel my passion and sharpen my focus on using every skill and opportunity at my disposal to drive meaningful change.

For instance, in areas with limited medical infrastructure, I've relied on the leadership and strategic planning abilities cultivated through my medical education to strengthen healthcare delivery systems. My goal is always to ensure that interventions are not only effective in the moment but also sustainable and culturally appropriate in the long term. This includes building capacity among local healthcare providers, improving access to medical supplies, and developing protocols that align with both global health standards and local realities.

The integration of my clinical expertise, nursing foundation, and leadership acumen has been instrumental in this mission. As my influence has expanded through hospital-based programs and global health initiatives, I've come to fully embrace that leadership in healthcare extends far beyond the walls of any one institution. It is about enabling communities to take ownership of their health. This often means mentoring healthcare workers in underserved regions, strengthening local health infrastructure, and advocating for systemic reforms that address social determinants such as poverty, education, and access to clean water.

Effective healthcare leadership is especially crucial in global health contexts, where resources are limited, and populations are disproportionately affected by disease, inequality, and geographic isolation. My experiences have shown me that leadership in these settings requires more than clinical knowledge—it demands cultural sensitivity, logistical agility, and the ability to collaborate across disciplines and borders. By combining my medical insights with lessons from the frontlines of leadership, I am better equipped to tackle complex challenges and help shape health systems that are inclusive, responsive, and resilient.

What I've learned is that the responsibilities of a healthcare leader are not confined to any single setting. The blend of my nursing roots, medical training, and leadership journey has prepared me to serve effectively both in hospitals and in humanitarian missions—each setting different, yet equally vital in its impact. Whether coordinating care in a modern clinical facility or helping to organize mobile clinics in remote areas, the heart of the work remains the same: compassion, integrity, and a commitment to serving others.

Healthcare is one of the few professions where your work can quite literally span continents—and touch lives in the most profound ways. As I continue this journey, I remain dedicated to addressing urgent health issues in both local and global communities, guided by the same values that have shaped my life and career: service, empathy, and the unwavering belief that everyone deserves access to compassionate, high-quality care.

FINDING 3 ONE PURPOSE

If you search for a definition of "life purpose," you will likely encounter more than one result.

The most common meaning of life purpose is the intention or motivation that drives a person to act—or refrain from acting—in order to achieve a state of supreme well-being.

In other words, we are talking about a goal, a purpose. It is the fuel that keeps you moving, motivates you to pursue one goal (and not another), and guides you toward your well-being.

It can mean several things, from happiness to health, or even service to others.

Call it whatever you like.

What is the first thing that comes to mind when you think about your life purpose? Is it clear to you, or are you still unsure? In both cases, you should know that this is not a fixed notion—nor is life itself. In other words, it can change as you transform.

Although we will present you with different examples of a life purpose, we want you to know that it is perfectly normal to still be questioning them. The important thing is that you start moving toward them. Maybe you already know them, but you're not yet aware.

A life purpose helps us focus on achieving personal goals that align with our current experiences because, as we've already mentioned, people are constantly changing—and with them, our projects and needs.

The purpose of life is created, and there can be more than one. It is not given in a predestined way. It requires you to prepare and be consistent with it. Do you want to start working on yours?

Mark Twain said there are two important days in the life of every human being. The first is when you are born, and the second is when you discover why you were born; that is when you finally understand your purpose in life.

When thinking about the purpose of life, people often refer to some kind of spiritual calling, where the religious doctrine they practice proposes a direction they must follow to get closer to spiritual fulfillment. While this is a valid argument, it is not the only one.

The purpose of life is what gives meaning to our existence. It is what encourages us to get out of bed every day. We all need something that motivates us to grow, seek new horizons, and overcome our limiting beliefs—to believe in our potential.

But there is something else about the purpose of life that not many people know: it can vary and be multiple. What is truly important is that you have a reason to use all the capacities for work and life that you have developed up to that moment for the common good.

Is having a productive life the same as having a life with purpose?

Purpose is not synonymous with productivity. However, in most cases, productivity can result from having discovered your purpose.

Productivity is a set of tangible actions that we perform day after day. It is understood that these are concrete tasks we carry out with measurable value into which we invest time. However, these productive tasks may or may not align with our purpose. That is why we may not feel committed or involved with our actions.

However, the purpose of life leads you to draw up a roadmap—a plan and a goal—that connects with the fulfillment of your objectives and desires. Therefore, each action we take in pursuit of that goal will be filled with motivation; we will feel good doing them, and we will be committed to ensuring that the results reflect the best we can give. While productive, we will be connected with well-being, joy, and a positive and healthy attitude. I think the difference is obvious.

How to Find Your Life Purpose to Live with Intention

If you've ever wondered, "Am I living life to the fullest?" "Am I doing what I'm passionate about?" or "What do I want out of life?" you're not alone. These universal questions invite us to reflect deeply on our existence and purpose.

Discovering your true purpose can fill you with energy, passion, and excitement for the future. That's why today, you'll learn how to determine whether you lack purpose in life and gain practical tools to identify and begin moving toward what you want.

"Finding your purpose" is a phrase often mentioned in different contexts, including life coaching sessions, work environments, and even therapy sessions. But what is a life purpose? A life purpose is an overall vision for your future based on the most meaningful things to you. It is often a central goal or set of goals that help you:

- Guide your decision-making
- Provide a specific address
- Giving meaning to your actions
- Determine how you prioritize your time

Life's purpose can be considered your "why," or the reason you get out of bed every morning. It is the motivating factor behind many things you do, shaping your goals and making you feel like you are in this world for a reason.

Importance of Having a Purpose in Life to Be Happier

The University of California conducted a study among 1,042 people between the ages of 21 and 100, concluding that the purpose of life should be considered a relevant clinical factor, as it increases well-being and promotes patient improvement.

Let's look at it from a simpler perspective, comparing the development of a life purpose with any objective, such as buying a car, going on vacation, or taking a workshop. We will find that the former gives order to our lives by guiding our actions.

For example, everything would make more sense if the course you want to take right now aligns with your life purpose, rather than doing it merely as a hobby or out of work obligation. Because yes, it is such an immense sphere that it can encompass every aspect of our existence.

Furthermore, on a psychological level, the purpose of life can help people transform the pain of a traumatic experience into actions that lead them to grow and, in turn, allow them to lend a helping hand to those going through similar situations.

In other words, a purpose in life is the fundamental basis for serving others. It can strengthen bonds of solidarity between people and propose solutions to conflicts that affect entire communities, which benefits the individual who carries out such initiatives in multiple ways.

This is because it has been proven that when a person finds a purpose in life and knows that their work will benefit others, their effort and knowledge can generate comfort and well-being for those who may not have the same advantages.

That is, a life purpose can fill the person who has it with emotions and feelings of positive connotation, which translates into a better quality of life and health for themselves because they understand themselves as someone useful to their society or community.

In addition, this same purpose in life gives you the strength to better deal with fear and uncertainty when they appear. Your reason for living provides solid arguments for believing in your potential to take on the challenges you face.

Questions That Help You Discover the Purpose of Life

Both the life purpose of an organization and that of a person provide an answer to the reason for one's existence, and this argument is purely individual because it is based on each person's unique and personal experiences.

This means that an individual with a similar life does not necessarily have the same purpose, just as a company in the same field does not have the same meaning or values as its competition. It is a very subjective notion marked by experiences and points of view.

While it is true that finding the purpose of life is a process whose complexity can vary for each individual, it never really ends because, as we mentioned before, there may be more than one purpose, and it may change over time.

However, a series of reflective questions can help you investigate your purpose in life. Keep in mind that this requires you to dedicate a reasonable amount of time to self-knowledge, and although the answer may not come concretely, it will help you to know more about yourself.

- ❖ What are my best skills?
- ❖ What do I enjoy doing most?
- ❖ What is my life maxim?
- ❖ What do I believe in?
- ❖ What activities make me feel good about myself?
- ❖ How can I be useful to others by putting my talents to work?
- ❖ What are my values and principles?
- ❖ What would I do if I had little time left to live?
- ❖ What would you do if you were a millionaire or had a position of responsibility and power?
- ❖ What do I spend my free time on?

Examples of a Life Purpose

Assuming you are still unsure how to start or what we are discussing, I want to share with you some simple examples of a life purpose, with which you will be able to see how a person can give meaning to their existence and turn it into a professional objective: Raise a family and be a good example for your children.

- ❖ Get actively involved in social causes, such as combating climate change. Do something that helps others through difficult times, leaving something good behind.
- ❖ Working on research to find better ways to cure diseases.
- ❖ Travel and get to know different places and cultures around the world.
- ❖ Hellen Keller was a deaf blind writer and activist who drew on her difficulties to create a purpose in life, which led her to become the first person with her condition to obtain a college degree. She transformed her adversities into her fuel to help and fight for the rights of others.
- ❖ Venezuelan marathon runner Maickel Melamed was born with a motor disability but still decided to pursue a university education. His life purpose led him to learn the benefits of public speaking and to use it to inspire others.
- ❖ Many young people dedicate themselves to studying medicine because they have lost a loved one to an illness such as cancer, and they want to find a cure to help heal other people.

According to Matthew 22:37–40, our purpose is to love God fully and our neighbors as ourselves. We are to *"live a radical life of obedience and love."*

It's good to remember that what you set out to do doesn't have to be something too ambitious or impossible. Your purpose can be anything because everyone finds meaning in different ways.

Understanding the Journey

Answering the question, "What is my purpose in life?" may seem simple, but doing so is challenging. The reality is that finding your purpose is a journey with ups and downs. At times, you may feel on top of the world, proud of everything you're doing and the difference you're making where it matters most. But at other times, you might feel discouraged and need to regain your purpose. So, know that feeling all this is normal and that there's always a way to get back on track.

Are you lacking purpose in life?

From a psychological perspective, the feeling of lacking purpose in life can be deeply destabilizing, affecting both our mental health and overall well-being. Lack of purpose can manifest itself in several psychological and emotional symptoms, including:

Decreased Energy: A persistent feeling of fatigue not relieved by rest, signaling a lack of intrinsic motivation.

Disinterest in the Future: Having difficulty visualizing or getting excited about the future can limit planning and hope for the future.

Feelings of Ineffectiveness: The belief that one is not contributing meaningfully can impact self-esteem and sense of self-worth.

Lack of Recognition of Achievements: An inability to see or value one's successes can fuel dissatisfaction and unworthiness.

Loss of Interest in Normally Pleasurable Activities: A clear indicator of demotivation that can border on anhedonia, a common symptom in mood disorders such as depression.

Although a psychologist coach can help you discover your purpose, if you have any of these symptoms, it would be advisable for you to seek psychological therapy instead of coaching.

Step by Step: How to Answer the Question, "What is My Purpose?"

If you're feeling discouraged about finding your purpose, there are some mental exercises and steps you can take to get closer to your true calling. Try thinking about them and writing down your initial thoughts as you go.

Identify Values

One of the most interesting concepts I encountered when I first became interested in personal development was values. The idea that your values represent what is truly important to you and that identifying yours can bring great clarity to your life seemed incredibly powerful. If you search the Internet for the meaning of the word "values," you will find definitions like:

Values are those principles, virtues, or qualities that characterize a person, an action, or an object and are typically considered positive or of great importance by a social group. Or values are the guidelines that each individual establishes to adapt them to their lifestyle, define their personality, meet goals, satisfy needs, and follow a list of positive actions.

I find these ways of explaining what values are too complex, abstract, and—in my opinion—not very accurate.

I would like to start this by sharing my understanding of this term. For me, values represent personal qualities or aspects of life.

For example, honor, respect, and generosity are values. But so are punctuality, determination, and having money. In addition to that, there are 3 important characteristics that values have and that you should know:

- ❖ Values have no objective meaning. Instead, we assign meaning to them based on our beliefs and experiences.

  So, what you understand by "justice" is probably different from what I understand and very different from what a Chinese understands.

- ❖ Values do not have a static meaning. Since what they represent depends on our beliefs, the meaning we give to our values evolves as we accumulate new experiences and our beliefs change.

That's why friendship doesn't mean the same thing to you now as it did when you were 13, and you don't understand health the same way before and after overcoming cancer.

- ❖ Values are not something you "either have or don't have." That is to say, it is incorrect to say that you "have" the value of creativity but "don't have" the value of respect.

You can say that a value is more or less present in your day-to-day life. Or that it is more or less important to you at this moment in your life. However, the reality is that all human beings "have" all the values because they all mean something to us; therefore, we have a relationship with them.

Even a very selfish person will "have" the value of generosity.

However, due to his beliefs or personal experiences, he does not practice it because he does not see it as necessary.

When you are born, your brain's "operating system" comes with an empty folder for each value: one for friendship, one for cooperation, one for determination...

As you age and gain experience, you keep your beliefs about the values they represent in each of these folders.

For example, if your parents were very hard on you when you were young to get good grades, you might add "Getting good grades is necessary to be successful in life" to the "scholarly success" folder.

However, suppose one day you do a favour for a friend who is having a hard time and a few months later, you need help, and that friend ignores you. In that case, you may end up creating in the "generosity" folder the file "If you are generous, others will take advantage of you," and in the "friendship" folder the file "Even your best friends can trick you when you least expect it."

In the end, the important thing is for you to understand that your hard drive comes "from the factory" with folders for all the values, that the meaning of each value depends on the files you have inside that folder, and that this meaning will change as you add, delete or modify those files.

A simple checklist on How I Identify My Values

- ❖ **Reflect on Meaningful Experiences:** I start by thinking about times when I felt deeply fulfilled, proud, or genuinely happy. These moments stand out because they usually align with my values, even if I wasn't fully aware of them. I note who was with me, what I was doing, and what made these experiences special. For instance, if I felt content while helping someone, it might signal that kindness or service is one of my values. Writing down these memories helps me notice patterns that reveal what truly matters to me.

- ❖ **Notice Patterns in My Life:** I look at the activities I naturally gravitate toward, whether in my free time, at work, or in my hobbies. If I consistently spend time creating or exploring, I might value creativity or adventure. Similarly, if I frequently prioritize family, it suggests relationships are central to my values. Observing these habits lets me see where I'm already honoring my values, often without realizing it.

- ❖ **Examine What Triggers Strong Emotions:** I pay attention to what stirs up strong feelings in me, both positive and negative. My reactions to certain situations—such as joy, frustration, or discomfort—often highlight my values. Suppose I'm bothered by dishonesty, for example. That tells me that integrity is important to me. Similarly, feeling uplifted by helping others might indicate compassion as a core value. I take note of these reactions to identify the underlying values that shape my emotional responses.

❖ **Identify Role Models and Admired Qualities:** I think about the people I admire, whether they're family, friends, or public figures, and consider what qualities I look up to in them. I ask myself why I'm drawn to these traits—like resilience, honesty, or generosity—since they often reflect the person I aspire to be. Looking at my role models helps me uncover values I want to embody myself, and these qualities can serve as a guide for my personal growth.

❖ **List Core Beliefs or Motivators:** I reflect on the beliefs that motivate me and give me direction, especially when making big decisions. These might include respecting everyone, striving for personal growth, or seeking adventure. I write down these guiding beliefs, which usually represent deeper values that shape my choices. Identifying these motivators brings clarity to what drives me forward each day.

❖ **Use a List of Common Values for Inspiration:** Sometimes, I look at common values to see what resonates. As I read each one, I ask myself whether it feels significant to me or if I could take it or leave it. If a word like "honesty" or "freedom" feels particularly important, I explore why that is. This practice helps me discover values I might not have thought of right away but that feel true to who I am.

- ❖ **Narrow Down to Top Values:** After gathering ideas, I narrow my list to five or ten values that feel most essential. I might respect many values, but this helps me focus on the ones shaping my decisions and perspectives. This clarity makes it easier for me to live intentionally and make choices that align with what's important. This list isn't final—it's more like a snapshot of what matters to me now.

- ❖ **Define Each Value in My Own Words:** I make each value personal by writing a quick definition in my own words. For instance, "integrity" might mean staying honest even when it's hard, or "adventure" might mean trying new things that push me out of my comfort zone. Defining them for myself adds depth to each value and makes it easier to see how it fits into my life and goals.

- ❖ **Test My Values in Real Life:** With my values in mind, I look at my daily routine and decisions to see if they line up with what's important to me. For example, if I value health but am constantly stressed, I might need to rethink my work-life balance. Testing my values doesn't mean I have to make big changes immediately, but it helps me see where small adjustments could help me feel more aligned and authentic. I can also recognize where my values already shine through, which can be reassuring.

- ❖ **Re-evaluate Periodically:** I understand that values can change over time, so I check in occasionally. Major life changes, like moving or changing careers, can shift what's important to me. Revisiting my values ensures I'm still aligned with what truly matters and helps me adjust if necessary. This way, I know I'm making the right choices for where I am.

Developing Goals and Dreams

Developing goals and dreams starts with having a clear vision of what you want in life and setting actionable steps to reach that vision. It's a process that requires self-reflection, planning, and commitment, but it's also about staying open to growth and change. Here's a way to approach it:

First, I think about what truly inspires me—those ideas or possibilities that feel exciting and meaningful. These are my big-picture aspirations that don't have to be realistic immediately. It could be something as large as wanting to make a difference in a particular field, living a certain lifestyle, or becoming an expert in something that fascinates me. Dreaming big and brainstorming without limitations helps me tap into a raw, personal vision that feels genuine. I ask myself, "What do I want to experience, achieve, or be known for?"

Next, I start breaking down these dreams into goals. Dreams are often broad, while goals make them concrete. For example, if my dream is to travel the world, a specific goal could be to save a set amount for a yearly trip. This step is about taking a dream and giving it structure. I'll ask questions like, "What does success look like for this dream?" and "What are smaller, achievable steps I can take?" Thinking through what I need to accomplish in the short, medium, and long term makes each goal feel possible, and each step brings me closer to my vision.

Setting goals often means making them specific, measurable, and time-bound, which makes it easier to track progress and stay motivated. For example, rather than saying, "I want to be healthier," I'd define a goal like, "I want to exercise three times a week for the next three months." This clarity helps me see where I am at any given point and adjust my approach as needed. Making goals achievable within my current resources and time is key because it keeps me motivated and reduces frustration.

I also consider that some goals may require building new skills or changing certain habits. Part of goal development is asking myself what to learn or improve to reach these goals. If a goal feels challenging or outside my comfort zone, I might need to practice patience and persistence. Breaking larger goals into smaller tasks or milestones keeps me from feeling overwhelmed and lets me celebrate progress, even if just completing one small task brings me closer to the larger goal.

A crucial part of goal-setting is regularly reviewing and adjusting my goals. Life can change, and so can my priorities. Checking in on my progress—monthly, quarterly, or annually—helps me stay on track and adapt as necessary. If I'm not progressing, it could mean I need a new approach, more resources, or maybe even a different goal. Being flexible with my dreams and goals doesn't mean giving up on them; it means being realistic and adapting to new circumstances. Growth often requires adjustments, and I keep my options open to recalibrate as I go.

Setting goals to achieve my dreams is a journey that involves discovering what I want, committing to the process, adapting along the way, and celebrating each win, however small. It's about creating an achievable plan aligned with my values, knowing that my dreams may evolve as I grow. This mindset keeps me focused, balanced, and excited about the future I'm building for myself.

What are your convictions or guide?

What truly shapes the foundation of my life? How does one find the principles that guide them through every trial, every joy, and every season? The answer lies in the purpose to serve, rooted in early experiences and lessons that have echoed through my life. Born into a family that valued responsibility, I was given the unusual task of handling money as a child—my father's "bank," as he called it. Looking back, I see how these small acts taught me about trust, stewardship, and the weight of responsibility. How can children truly understand what they are being taught when they're told, "This month, set this money aside for food," or "Save this for your brother's school fees"? At the time, I thought it was merely a game, but now I realize it was my father's way of teaching me discipline, budgeting, and commitment. Isn't it remarkable how, even in youth, seeds of wisdom can be planted, growing into the very essence of who we become?

And then there was my mother, whose unwavering faith in the face of hardship taught me resilience. I remember her carrying me for hours to the nearest hospital when illness nearly took my life—against the advice of those who had already given up hope. How many people have someone who will go to such lengths, carrying them when they are too weak to walk alone? In that moment, my mother's determination became my own, a beacon that reminds me never to give up, even when others say it's impossible. Her prayer by my bedside, pleading for my life, was a gift—a promise that I would carry forward. Isn't it true that the strength of those who raise us becomes the foundation we stand on?

But what of my path, shaped by years of education and work, of dreams pursued and adapted? I moved across continents, chasing opportunities and building a life. Each new step—studying nursing, becoming a registered nurse, and becoming a healthcare leader—brought challenges. Yet the calling to serve remained constant. As I advanced in my career, even moments in leadership positions became lessons in humility and dedication to others. Do these roles define me, or is it the purpose behind them that truly matters? My belief in serving others took root in these experiences, growing stronger with each encounter with patients and colleagues who relied on me. Service became more than an action; it became a purpose that wove through every aspect of my life.

When I lost my husband and moved back to be with my children, life's fragility became unmistakable. It forced me to look deeper and ask what remained when all roles and titles disappeared. What if my calling has always been to make a meaningful difference—not just as a mother or wife but as a person committed to lifting others? I realized that my purpose didn't lie in the roles themselves, but in the impact, I could make on people's lives. Isn't purpose something that must transcend titles and accomplishments?

Serving others is my guiding star—the belief that no matter what I face, my purpose remains steady: to make a difference in whatever way I can. And so, I wonder, isn't life richer when we use it to serve? This purpose is not a task or duty; it is the heartbeat of my life, and I know that as long as I am here, I will continue to live by this conviction. What greater purpose could there be?

What are your core values?
Expanding on these values reveals the deeper layers and how they intertwine, creating a foundation that guides my decisions and how I view life and interact with those around me. Compassion, for example, isn't just a feeling of empathy—it's an action, a responsibility to contribute positively to others' lives. I believe compassion builds bridges, bringing understanding where there might be division. In a world where empathy often takes a backseat to self-interest, how powerful is it to consciously choose kindness? Compassion teaches me that every person I encounter is fighting their own battles. It asks me to be gentle with my words, patient with my actions, and present for those who need support. Whether it's a family member, a friend, or even a

stranger, compassion pushes me to listen more than I speak and to offer a helping hand without waiting for something in return. Isn't life enriched when we approach each other with a mindset that seeks to understand rather than judge?

Integrity brings a sense of grounding to everything I do. Integrity means upholding honesty and authenticity, even when taking shortcuts or presenting a façade would be easier. I've learned that integrity shouldn't be adjusted based on convenience—it's an unyielding commitment. Integrity shapes how I move through relationships, careers, and personal goals. It reminds me that my reputation and self-respect are built on every decision I make. Imagine living in a way where every action aligns with your values, knowing that your word is something others can trust. Isn't there immense peace in knowing that you don't have to hide behind half-truths or constantly worry about the image you portray? In this sense, integrity isn't just for others—it's also for myself, a promise to remain genuine in a world that often rewards appearances over substance.

With resilience, I've seen life's challenges as chapters in my personal growth story rather than barriers. Resilience is the inner strength that pushes me to rise each time I stumble, to find new ways forward, and to learn through hardship. Life's setbacks, though painful, have taught me adaptability and patience. They have shown me that sometimes the greatest lessons come from difficult experiences. When I face hardship, I remind myself that this will pass and that I will emerge stronger and more capable. Resilience isn't about avoiding pain—it's about embracing it and using it to fuel growth. How would we know our strength if we never faced adversity? Every time I overcome an obstacle, I become more certain of my ability to handle whatever life brings, and that certainty reinforces all of my other values.

Growth is a value that pushes me toward constant self-improvement. I see growth as a lifelong journey involving learning new skills and deepening my understanding. Growth keeps me humble; it reminds me that there is always more to learn and that every person I meet and every experience I encounter has something valuable to teach me. I stay open-minded, curious, and engaged with the world by embracing growth. It's easy to settle into routines and familiar patterns, but true growth often happens outside our comfort zones. Am I truly living if I remain stagnant—if I refuse to evolve? Growth answers that question, propelling me toward a fuller, richer life.

Service is the value that ties everything together. True fulfillment comes from making a difference in others 'lives and using my abilities and time to lift others. Service is about giving without expecting anything in return—a way of contributing to the greater good. Whether volunteering, mentoring, or simply being there for someone in need, service brings purpose to my life. It shifts the focus from "What can I gain?" to "What can I give?" In moments of doubt or difficulty, service reminds me of the larger picture—that my life is part of a bigger tapestry where every small action can create positive change. Isn't life most meaningful when we dedicate ourselves to something greater than personal gain?

Altogether, these values are my compass. They shape how I perceive challenges, how I interact with others, and how I define success. Through compassion, I connect with others; through integrity, I remain true to myself; through resilience, I navigate life's difficulties; through growth, I continue to expand my horizons; and through service, I contribute to something beyond myself. Living by these values doesn't mean I'm always perfect or never struggle, but it gives me a foundation I can rely on. Whenever life's path becomes unclear, these values offer clarity, helping me realign with the person I strive to be. And I ask myself, is there a greater satisfaction than knowing each day is spent pursuing what I truly believe in? With these values at the core of who I am, I feel equipped to face whatever comes my way, knowing I am building a true, meaningful, and deeply fulfilling life.

Six Ways to Build Your Life Purpose

It is important that while you discover your life purpose, you focus on strengthening or developing skills that can help you grow as a person and as a professional. For this reason, we have made some courses and training available to you that can greatly help.

Use the Japanese technique of ikigai

The Japanese term ikigai doesn't have an exact translation into English. However, its concept can be summed up as "reason for being" or "reason for getting up in the morning." It is a purpose in life. For people born into this culture, everyone has a reason to live.

In recent years, this notion has been used in the Western world to help people find meaning in their existence so they can live fully, as shown in the Academy of Emotions. For this, ikigai must be built on four pillars.

These are passion, mission, profession, and calling. What you love to do encompasses your passion and mission; what you do well is based on your passion and profession; what you can obtain financial compensation for through your profession and calling; and what is needed is your mission and calling.

Think that your life purpose can be multiple

As we mentioned a couple of paragraphs ago, you don't necessarily need to have a single reason for living because the reasons why a person wants to live fully and go out and give their best every day can be diverse.

You have the potential to expand. Suppose you still haven't found your reason for being. In that case, you can think of the various scenarios in which your knowledge, skills, and abilities can greatly help in different areas and by carrying out different actions.

We all play different roles in our lives. A person may be a computer technician but also like to teach computing to people with limited resources, give private lessons, and engage in academic research in the area.

Surround yourself with people who inspire you to grow
Our social nature makes us feed off and copy the attitudes of those around us. Choose to be with people who push you to go further, encourage you to achieve your goals, and, with their own life stories, are a model for you.

This will motivate you and give you the inner vigor to pursue your dreams. This tool can help you understand what motivates you most daily, what moves you to act, and what activities make you happy.

Furthermore, having friends who motivate you can also be the perfect excuse to expand your circle of friends because, generally, people who are satisfied with their life goals are surrounded by people who are on the same wavelength as them.

You can find it in limiting or unjust situations

But just as we find meaning in our existence by doing what we love, we can also find meaning in traumatic situations that have changed our lives forever. This can be a deeply healing experience. You would need your shortcomings, obstacles, and what others would see as weaknesses as your greatest strength to support and motivate other people.

So, we suggest that you also think about those situations of injustice that have affected you and your obstacles in life, or perhaps that you use what a loved one has experienced to raise awareness about the issue, propose solutions, or at least ease the burdens of others.

Develop a life decree

A simple way to start is by writing a text expressing where you see yourself in the future—a vision of what you want to do and how to achieve it. In this way, you will be able to organize your plans and goals to channel them toward that future.

Of course, it is worth remembering that your vision must be flexible and that it is okay to make adjustments and change plans because life flows, and with it, so do we. It is impossible to conceive of human existence as something immutable because, as humans, we are constantly changing.

Once you have that vision on paper, it would be a good idea to write down some affirmative sentences that support that idea of the future—that is, an intention that motivates you to go down that path, that mentally prepares you so that you can focus and achieve your goals.

Give a focus on service to others
Mother Teresa of Calcutta said those who do not live to serve are not fit to live. She mentioned the need for all human beings to feel useful to others because our lives gain meaning when we know that what we do helps others.

Whatever your abilities, you can put them to the service of others in your community to generate well-being. Remember what we told you about ikigai? Whether you profit or not, doing our bit is important.

Even if you are not professionally dedicated to a social cause, you can provide relief to others.

Volunteering is one of the most beautiful experiences anyone can have because it can help create a more just world—or at least a less harsh one—for those most in need.
Stop worrying if you don't have a defined purpose in life yet. The important thing is that you start asking yourself questions about yourself, that you inquire about your capabilities, about the

obstacles you have overcome to get to where you are. That's a good start.

Yes, it would be great if what you do was complementary to social service, but sometimes that doesn't happen. You don't need to be in a non-governmental organization to change the world. Perhaps there are people around you who need a helping hand.

Think about how what you know and are good at can benefit others. Of course, you can always donate money, but believe us— giving meaning to life and showing love to others through your work is a very satisfying experience.

CHALLENGES OF
4
PURPOSEFUL LIVING

L iving a purposeful life brings fulfillment, but it's often met with real challenges that test one's commitment. External pressures, like societal expectations and career demands, can pull us from our true goals, while fear of failure and self-doubt can create hesitation. Maintaining long-term motivation, resisting comparison to others, and balancing personal purpose with daily

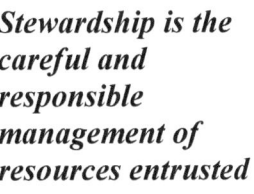

Stewardship is the careful and responsible management of resources entrusted to us.

responsibilities are ongoing struggles. These challenges, though difficult, offer chances for growth and resilience, ultimately making the pursuit of a meaningful life both rewarding and transformative.

Being a Good Steward of Your Resources

The concept of stewardship is a biblical principle that reminds us that everything we have is a gift from God, and as such, we are called to manage these resources responsibly.

Stewardship is the careful and responsible management of resources entrusted to us. As Christians, we believe that all of our resources—including our time, talents, treasures, and even our environment—come from God. Therefore, we are called to use these resources wisely, recognizing that they are not ours to waste or abuse.

Have you ever heard the phrase "time is money?" Although time is a resource, we all have, it is up to each person to decide how they use the 24 hours in their day.

Being a Good Steward of Our Time

Time management is considered a soft skill and is one of the most sought-after in the working world. It is so valuable because it not only makes you a more efficient person but also helps you do better-quality work and progress more quickly.

One of the most valuable resources we have is time. We only have a limited amount of time on this earth and must use it wisely. We can be good stewards of our time by prioritizing what is truly important in life. This means setting goals and using our time in a way that aligns with our values and beliefs. We can also use our time to serve others and contribute positively to our communities and the world around us.

Tips to manage your time and be more efficient

1. Set goals and prioritize

It is important to define which objectives are short, medium, and long-term. If you have an important work deadline due in a month and you do not manage your time beforehand, it will most likely catch you by surprise, and you will have to do things at the last minute.

The ideal way to set your goals is with the SMART methodology. Once this is done, you will determine the priority level of each one according to the deadline, level of difficulty, and importance for your life.

2. Visualize your activities

Whether in a planner, notes on your cell phone, your calendar, or your notebook, it's important to keep track of your daily, weekly, or monthly activities in a visible place. If you get into the habit of reading them, it will be easier to remember them in the future without having to check your planner constantly.

An additional tip is to use graphic resources such as colors, symbols, tables, and diagrams, as they will help you structure your ideas and communicate and execute them better. The Gantt chart is one of the most commonly used tools for this.

3. Create a routine

No one likes to feel stuck in a routine, so it's important to create one that suits your personality and lifestyle. If you like to fill your day with activities, getting up early will be key to achieving this.

You should also consider taking breaks in your routine and not doing one activity after another. Even though you want to make the most of your time, this is not the best way. Ideally, the largest percentage of your routine time should be for you, so think: is this routine for me or others?

4. Take advantage of technology

Thanks to great technological advances, there are programs, software, and templates that help us carry out everyday tasks and work more quickly. For work, there are tools that generate automatic reports. For household tasks, you can use smart devices that act as your virtual assistant and remind you of your daily activities.

5. Start delegating tasks

We must consider the following: Will it be easier or faster to do this if I work as a team? Can I ask or pay someone else to do it for me? Be careful—we are not paying someone to do your tasks or forcing someone to fulfill your responsibilities.

If you work and have to care for your children, perhaps the best idea is to hire a babysitter to help you for a few hours. Or if you are a person who is busy all day and likes to use your free time to relax, a good option is to hire someone to help you with household chores.

6. Limit your time and avoid postponing tasks

We will always enjoy some tasks more than others, and it is normal to want to spend a little more time on them. However, to properly complete everything, it is important to designate a specific time for each one and, once completed, move on to the next. If our minds remain trapped in the previous activity, we cannot move forward efficiently for the rest of our day, and many of the tasks will likely be postponed until another day.

7. Take advantage of "dead time"

Despite having a structured schedule, we must maintain some flexibility, as priorities can change from one moment to the next, or even some free spaces can become available that we had not planned for. If you have something pending, take advantage of this time to complete it, or designate the time for some activity such as going to the gym, visiting your family, or advancing some personal or professional project.

8. Learn to say no

Finally, saying no is a skill that is acquired when we learn to prioritize our time. It is common for people to come to you for help or seek to delegate a task to you, but out of shame, we take time away from ourselves to do things for others. You should think carefully about whether the task you are about to accept will make it difficult to achieve your goals. Even if you have already said yes to something and realize that it is difficult to do, there is nothing wrong with changing your mind.

Being a Good Steward of Our Talents

Each of us has unique talents, strengths, and abilities meant to be nurtured, shared, and used to make a difference in the world. Imagine, for a moment, seeing every one of these gifts not merely as personal assets but as tools for positive impact—tools we've been entrusted with to uplift others and contribute to something greater than ourselves. This, my friends, is what it means to be a good steward of our talents.

Being a steward of talent starts with truly recognizing and valuing the gifts we've been given. Maybe you're a natural leader, a creative thinker, a problem-solver, or someone who just knows how to listen and connect. Whatever your talent may be, stewardship means understanding that this gift has purpose, potential, and power when used thoughtfully. It's about cultivating and continuously developing and refining these skills so they grow stronger, sharper, and more impactful. Talents are like seeds that need nurturing to reach their full potential, and each of us is responsible for investing in them and committing to that journey of growth.

But being a steward of talent doesn't stop at self-improvement. True stewardship is about looking outward and using what we've been given to serve others. It's about asking ourselves, "How can my abilities benefit those around me? How can I use this gift to bring support, joy, or inspiration?" This could mean lending a hand to someone in need, creating something that inspires, or even stepping up to lead in ways that make a difference. Stewardship transforms talents into gifts for the world that strengthen communities, build connections, and leave a lasting legacy. When we use our talents with a purpose beyond ourselves, we create a ripple effect, inspiring others to step forward and share their gifts.

And let's talk about gratitude. When we appreciate the talents we've been given, we are naturally inclined to use them well—to treat them as something valuable, something not to be wasted. Gratitude fuels stewardship. It keeps us grounded, reminding us that every ability and skill is something to honor and share. This gratitude, this appreciation, encourages us to put our talents to work thoughtfully, ensuring that each action we take is driven by a desire to give back, make a positive mark, and leave the world a little better than we found it.

Being a good steward of our talents is about legacy. It's about recognizing that the real measure of success is not simply what we achieve for ourselves but how we contribute to the lives of others. By committing to this journey and using our talents to serve, inspire, and uplift, we build a future that values generosity, integrity, and connection. We become part of something bigger than ourselves—something lasting.

Let us each commit to being good stewards of our talents. Let's embrace the potential within us and use it to make a difference, light up the lives of others, and create a world where everyone's gifts can shine.

Being Good Stewards of Our Treasures

Being a good steward of our treasures involves treating our resources—time, money, possessions, and talents—with respect, gratitude, and purpose. Here are some practical steps to help guide this approach.

Budget Wisely and Live Within Your Means: Take an honest look at your finances, create a budget, and stick to it. Living within your means ensures you're not overextending yourself financially and helps prevent debt. This allows for peace of mind and greater freedom to share your resources.

Avoid Unnecessary Debt: Debt can limit your freedom to manage your finances effectively. While some debt (like a mortgage or educational loans) may be necessary, unnecessary debt can add stress. Aim to save and pay in cash or prioritize paying down any existing debts when possible.

Cultivate Generosity: Being a good steward means recognizing that resources can be shared. Regularly give to causes or people in need. This might be through charitable donations, supporting local organizations, or helping someone directly in your community. Generosity doesn't have to be grand; small, consistent acts can create lasting change and fulfillment.

Maintain What You Own: Protect your belongings to extend their lifespan. Regularly maintaining your possessions, such as your home, car, and other valuable items, helps prevent unnecessary replacements and promotes sustainability. It also encourages gratitude for what you already have rather than focusing on acquiring more.

Use Resources Wisely: Adopt a mindful approach to consumption. Avoid impulse buying and consider whether new purchases are truly needed. This approach helps save money and reduces waste, benefiting your finances and the environment.

Give Your Time and Skills: Stewardship goes beyond money and possessions. Volunteering your time, sharing your skills, or mentoring others are meaningful ways to give back. Time and knowledge are often the most impactful gifts we can offer, and they create deep connections with others.

Plan for the Future: Set goals for the future, both financially and personally. Saving and investing wisely can prepare you for unexpected expenses and help you reach your long-term goals. This could be setting aside funds for retirement, emergencies, or educational goals, which provides security and allows you to support yourself and others.

Practice Gratitude: Being grateful for what you have shifted the focus from wanting more to appreciating enough. This mindset often leads to more mindful decisions around spending, giving, and caring for possessions. Gratitude encourages us to view everything as a blessing to be respected and valued.

Involve Your Family: If possible, involve your family in your stewardship journey. Teaching children or discussing financial responsibility and the importance of giving with a partner can help build a foundation of responsible habits and values that last across generations.

Stay Accountable: Reflect on your actions and decisions regularly. Having someone to discuss your goals and progress with or journaling about your stewardship journey can help keep you grounded and consistent in your intentions.

These practices allow us to be mindful of how we handle our resources, creating habits that serve us and others in the long term. By stewarding our treasures, we honour our blessings, build a meaningful life, and positively impact the world.

Being a Good Stewards of the Environment

Being good stewards of the environment means recognizing our responsibility to care for the planet. It's about making choices that protect and preserve natural resources so future generations can enjoy and benefit from them. This involves being conscious of how we use resources—such as water, energy, and materials—and ensuring we are not wasteful. Small changes in our daily lives can collectively make a significant difference. For example, reducing plastic use, conserving water, and recycling whenever possible are small but impactful actions that help decrease pollution and protect ecosystems.

Reducing waste is another key aspect of environmental stewardship. When we minimize the amount of waste we produce, we help reduce landfill overflow and lower the demand for resource-intensive production. Simple habits, like opting for reusable products instead of disposable ones, can dramatically decrease the waste each person generates. Composting food scraps, for example, is a great way to reduce landfill contributions and even create nutrient-rich soil for plants, which supports local ecosystems.

Supporting sustainable practices is also a powerful way to make a positive environmental impact. This can mean purchasing products from companies that prioritize eco-friendly practices, choosing locally produced foods, or supporting renewable energy initiatives. These choices help shift demand toward environmentally conscious production, which can reduce pollution, conserve resources, and promote biodiversity. Additionally, buying locally reduces the need for long-distance transportation, which helps cut down on greenhouse gas emissions.

By actively caring for the environment, we protect the earth and show appreciation for the incredible diversity of life and natural beauty. Respecting and nurturing the environment honors the world we have been given and reflects a sense of gratitude for all it provides. Simple acts, like planting trees, cleaning up natural spaces, or conserving water, connect us with nature and remind us of our role in preserving it. As stewards, we must maintain this precious resource, knowing that each small step contributes to a healthier planet and a better future.

Being a Light to Others in the Dark

Being a light to others in a world that can sometimes feel dark involves intentional actions and a compassionate mindset. Living purposefully and striving to be a beacon of light in a world that often feels overwhelming, chaotic, or dark presents a unique set of challenges. The goal of being a positive influence in the lives of others requires a deep sense of personal commitment and resilience. It involves striving to live with authenticity and empathy and upholding values that can inspire and support those around us. Here are some of the main aspects and hurdles associated with this path.

Practice Kindness in Small Acts: Simple gestures like offering a genuine compliment, helping someone with a task, or listening without judgment can brighten someone's day. Small acts of kindness can create a positive ripple effect, encouraging others to pay it forward.

Stay Positive but Authentic: Rather than pretending everything is perfect, share your optimism while acknowledging challenges. Be the person who offers hope, focusing on solutions and resilience without dismissing others' experiences.

Be a Source of Encouragement and Support: Let people know they are not alone. Offer words of encouragement, be there to listen, and celebrate others' successes. Sometimes, just being present can provide comfort.

Share Your Knowledge and Skills: If you have specific skills or knowledge, use them to help others. Whether tutoring, giving advice, or helping with tasks, sharing knowledge can empower others and inspire confidence.

Lead by Example: Live with integrity, honesty, and respect for others. Demonstrate empathy, patience, and humility in your actions, encouraging those around you to follow suit. Your actions can inspire more effectively than words alone.

Be Patient and Understanding: Everyone struggles, and offering understanding without judgment can help others feel safe and valued. See situations from others' perspectives and respond empathetically, even in challenging interactions.

Practice Gratitude Publicly: Show gratitude and encourage others to do the same. This can shift focus to the positive aspects of life and uplift people around you. Gratitude is contagious and can help others see the light in their lives.

Volunteer and Get Involved in Community Service: Giving time to support those in need is a tangible way to spread light. Whether through organized charities or small neighborhood initiatives, giving back can create a real impact.

Stay Informed but Centered: While aware of world events is essential, avoid letting negative news consume you. Instead, stay grounded and focus on what you can control, inspiring others to remain hopeful and resilient.

Be Open About Your Struggles and Growth: When appropriate, share how you've overcome challenges. This honesty can help others feel less alone and show them it's possible to overcome difficult times.

Create Safe Spaces for Others to Share: Being a trusted confidant or creating an environment where people feel comfortable sharing their struggles can provide relief. Listen actively, validate their feelings, and provide support without trying to "fix" everything.

Set Boundaries and Encourage Self-Care: Taking care of yourself is essential to helping others effectively. Show that setting boundaries and practicing self-care is not selfish but necessary so you can continue to offer support without depleting yourself.

Promote Hope and Resilience in Conversations: When discussing fears or doubts, offer perspectives highlighting resilience and encouraging a hopeful outlook. Instead of denying challenges, help others focus on their strengths and potential paths forward.

Be Patient with Your Impact: Understand that being a light in a dark world isn't always about instant results. Stay consistent in your actions, trust in the value of your efforts, and remember that even small changes can have a lasting impact on others.

Being a Peacemaker in Your Relationship

Being a peacemaker in relationships is about more than just avoiding conflict. It involves actively seeking harmony and reconciliation, and it's a crucial quality for anyone striving for meaningful and healthy relationships. The Bible emphasizes the importance of peacemaking, especially in Jesus 'words from Matthew 5:9: "Blessed are the peacemakers, for they will be called children of God." This powerful message suggests that being a peacemaker is not only rewarding in our personal lives but also aligns us with the values that God cherishes. True peacemaking is about understanding, forgiveness, humility, and taking responsibility for our actions within our relationships.

The Inevitable Nature of Conflict
Peacemaking becomes essential when we realize that conflicts are inevitable. As unique individuals, we bring our perspectives, beliefs, and personalities into every relationship. Whether with family, friends, or partners, it's natural for these differences to lead to occasional misunderstandings or disagreements. Yet, our approach to resolving these conflicts shapes the strength of our connections. Peacemaking allows us to honor God, respect others, and foster personal growth—creating relationships that are not only resilient but deeply fulfilling.

Seeking to Understand Before Being Understood
One foundational principle of peacemaking is the commitment to seek understanding before being understood. Proverbs 18:2 reminds us of the importance of prioritizing understanding over self-expression: *"Fools find no pleasure in understanding but delight in airing their own opinions."* In a peacemaker's approach,

this means listening actively and showing empathy toward the other person's feelings and perspectives. By setting aside personal judgments and focusing on what the other person is experiencing, we build a bridge of mutual respect that makes resolving conflicts easier and more constructive.

Speaking the Truth in Love

Another core element of peacemaking is speaking the truth in love. Ephesians 4:15 encourages us to communicate honestly but with gentleness: *"Instead, speaking the truth in love, we will grow to become in every respect the mature body of him who is the head, that is, Christ."* Rather than avoiding difficult conversations or glossing over issues, peacemakers address them directly, intending to strengthen—not tear down. It involves carefully choosing words that reflect love and respect, even when discussing challenging or painful topics. Speaking truth in love builds trust and fosters openness, creating an environment where everyone feels safe expressing themselves.

The Power of Forgiveness

Forgiveness is also essential to being a peacemaker. In Colossians 3:13, we find the guidance, *"Bear with each other and forgive one another if any of you has a grievance against someone. Forgive as the Lord forgave you."* Forgiveness does not imply excusing hurtful behavior or forgetting it altogether; rather, it's about releasing the hold past grievances have over us and allowing the relationship to move forward. By forgiving others as we have been forgiven, we show love and compassion that pave the way for deeper bonds and lasting peace. Forgiveness is a conscious choice that allows us to live freely without resentment.

Humility in Apologizing and Making Amends

Humility is also crucial in peacemaking, which includes being willing to apologize and make amends. James 5:16 reminds us, "Therefore confess your sins to each other and pray for each other so that you may be healed." It takes courage to admit when we've made mistakes, but doing so shows humility and a desire to heal any harm caused. Apologies should be genuine and, where possible, accompanied by efforts to make amends. This willingness to own up to our faults and take action to make things right strengthens trust and respect in any relationship.

Living as Peacemakers and Children of God

Being a peacemaker means choosing understanding, compassion, honesty, and humility over self-interest and pride. While peacemaking may not eliminate all conflicts, it equips us to handle them in ways that honor God and those around us. Embodying these principles brings peace into our lives and relationships, meaningfully impacting those around us. Through peacemaking, we contribute to a world where love, understanding, and kindness have the final word—truly living as children of God.

Building a Legacy of Faith and Service

Building a legacy of faith and service is about creating a life that reflects your beliefs and leaves a meaningful impact on those around you. It involves intentionally shaping how you want to be remembered, prioritizing values like compassion, integrity, and kindness. By weaving faith and service into daily life, you create a foundation that influences others positively and continues to inspire long after you're gone. This legacy is not about wealth or fame, but about how your actions and principles guide others— helping them find purpose, strength, and direction.

Faith as the Foundation of Legacy

A lasting legacy begins with a deep, committed faith. Hebrews 11:1 teaches that faith is the assurance of things hoped for and the conviction of things not seen. Faith acts as the core of purposeful living. To build a legacy rooted in faith, prioritize time with God. Prayer, Bible reading, and participation in a faith community strengthen this foundation. These practices help clarify values and set meaningful intentions, giving your legacy a spiritual purpose that can inspire others.

The Role of Service in Building Legacy

Service is faith in action. Jesus Himself highlighted the importance of serving others, stating in Mark 10:45 that He came *"not to be served, but to serve."* When we serve, we choose to put others' needs alongside our own. Whether through volunteering, supporting friends and family, or showing kindness in daily interactions, service creates a lasting impact. It shapes your legacy into one defined by empathy, humility, and love.

Everyday Acts of Service

Building a legacy of service doesn't require grand gestures. It often lives in small, everyday acts of generosity and compassion. Holding a door, offering a listening ear, or helping someone without expecting anything in return are powerful ways to serve. Approaching life with a spirit of service not only enhances relationships but creates meaningful moments others remember and carry forward. These simple acts have a ripple effect, inspiring others to serve as well.

Leading by Example

A powerful legacy is built by leading through example. People often remember how they felt around someone who embodied faith and kindness. Demonstrating honesty, respect, and consistency in your values inspires others to follow suit. This influence isn't achieved through words alone—it's shown through how you live. Leading by example ensures that your legacy speaks louder than words and leaves a lasting impression on everyone you encounter.

Focusing on What Truly Matters

Aligning your actions and priorities with what matters most is essential in building a legacy. Reflect on the values you want to be known for, and focus your time and resources on what reflects those beliefs. Whether it's time with loved ones, supporting causes close to your heart, or mentoring others, these efforts reinforce the foundation of your legacy and reveal the principles that define your life.

Passing Down Values to Future Generations

A legacy of faith and service isn't just for the present—it's meant to guide future generations. Pass down your values through storytelling, tradition, and mentorship. Share your beliefs with your family, friends, and mentees. Teach the importance of faith, kindness, perseverance, and resilience. When others witness you living out your values, they are more likely to carry those values forward, ensuring your legacy continues to grow and inspire.

Living with Purpose and Intention

Living a life of faith and service means making purposeful decisions every day. Be intentional about how you spend your time, use your voice, and offer your support. Let your daily actions reflect your commitment to faith and service. This intentional living builds a legacy of depth and meaning—one rooted in love, community, and divine purpose.

Building a legacy of faith and service is a lifelong commitment to living in a way that uplifts others and honors your beliefs. By prioritizing faith, embracing service, and leading by example, you create a legacy that resonates with purpose and continues to inspire others. Your actions today can influence generations, making your life a testimony to the values of faith, kindness, and compassion. By embracing this path, you contribute to a world where your legacy brings hope, strength, and inspiration to those who follow in your footsteps.

Choosing to Be Grateful in All Circumstances

Choosing gratitude, especially during life's challenges, is one of the most impactful ways to shape a positive outlook and influence others. Gratitude isn't only about appreciating the good times—it's about finding purpose and lessons in difficult situations. When we choose to be grateful, we cultivate a mindset that recognizes value in each experience, regardless of the outcome. This perspective helps us stay grounded, encourages resilience, and reinforces a sense of peace and contentment. By embracing gratitude, we build a legacy of strength and positivity that influences those around us, showing them the power of finding joy and appreciation even in less-than-ideal situations.

The Power of Gratitude

Gratitude is transformative—it can change how we view both life's challenges and its blessings. In Philippians 4:6-7, we're reminded to present our requests to God with thanksgiving, so that His peace may guard our hearts. Gratitude shifts our focus from what's lacking to what we already have, creating a sense of abundance even in difficulty. This change in perspective helps us maintain hope, build emotional resilience, and strengthen our mental well-being. By actively focusing on daily blessings, we uplift ourselves and those around us.

Finding Gratitude in Daily Life

Gratitude can be found in the simplest aspects of our daily routines. From waking up each morning to sharing a quiet moment with a loved one, we're surrounded by blessings—many of which we overlook. Gratitude practice can include journaling, offering thanks out loud, or simply pausing to reflect. When we intentionally appreciate these small moments, we build a habit of joy and contentment that reshapes how we engage with life. Over time, gratitude becomes a lens through which we see the world—full of value, even in the mundane.

Gratitude During Difficult Times

One of the greatest tests of gratitude is practicing it during hardships. It's natural to focus on pain or loss when things go wrong, but gratitude can offer stability in the storm. Choosing gratitude in tough times doesn't mean ignoring reality—it means recognizing that growth, support, or unseen blessings may still exist in the midst of struggle. This choice provides strength and clarity. It helps us move through difficulty with hope, reminding us that no moment is wasted when we can find meaning within it.

Expressing Gratitude to Others

Gratitude isn't just personal—it strengthens our connections with others. Expressing thanks builds relationships rooted in appreciation and respect. Saying "thank you," writing a note, or simply acknowledging someone's kindness can uplift and encourage them. These acts foster trust and positivity, creating a ripple effect of generosity and goodwill. When people feel seen and appreciated, they're more likely to continue showing up with compassion, deepening our sense of community and belonging.

Choosing Gratitude in Times of Uncertainty

Uncertainty can stir fear and anxiety, but gratitude anchors us in the present. When we focus on what we still have—relationships, breath, opportunities—we reduce the power of fear. Gratitude shifts our focus from what we can't control to what we can: our attitude and our responses. This grounded mindset offers peace, providing emotional shelter during unstable times. It doesn't erase the unknown, but it strengthens our resolve to face it with faith and courage.

The Impact of a Grateful Mindset

A consistent practice of gratitude enhances emotional, mental, and even physical health. Studies have shown that grateful individuals experience lower stress, improved sleep, stronger relationships, and greater overall happiness. Gratitude rewires our brains toward positivity, helping us see opportunity where we once saw obstacles. By living with gratitude, we not only enrich our own lives but model a powerful mindset that inspires others to do the same. The ripple effect of a grateful heart can shape families, communities, and even generations.

Gratitude as a Foundation for Faith and Service

Gratitude fuels both faith and service. When we truly appreciate our blessings, we naturally want to share them. This abundance mindset encourages acts of generosity, service, and kindness. It drives us to give back—not from obligation, but from joy. A grateful heart sees needs and responds with love. By tying gratitude to faith and service, we live out a legacy that is not only positive but purposeful—anchored in love, compassion, and humility.

Living a Life of Gratitude

To live a life of gratitude is to live a life of purpose, strength, and hope. Gratitude is a choice—a daily practice that shapes how we experience the world and how we're remembered. When we respond to both triumph and trial with thanksgiving, we teach others to appreciate their own journey. A life marked by gratitude leaves behind a legacy of joy and resilience, inviting future generations to embrace every moment with open hearts.

Embracing Challenges as Opportunities for Growth

Life often presents us with obstacles that can feel overwhelming, but these moments also offer powerful opportunities for growth and self-discovery. Embracing challenges doesn't mean ignoring our struggles—it means recognizing them as part of our journey toward becoming stronger, wiser, and more compassionate. When we approach hardships with a mindset focused on learning, we build resilience and open ourselves to transformation. In doing so, we live more purposefully, cultivating a life defined not by comfort, but by courage and character.

Seeing problems as opportunities shifts our perspective. Instead of avoiding adversity, we lean into it, knowing that growth often arises from discomfort. This shift can change how we live—and how others perceive our journey.

Building Resilience Through Adversity

Adversity teaches us resilience—the inner strength that enables us to rise after falling. Life's most difficult seasons can reveal our capacity to endure, adapt, and continue moving forward. Resilience doesn't mean we're unaffected by pain; it means we learn to stand firm in the midst of it. With each challenge we face, we gain confidence in our ability to persevere. Over time, resilience becomes a core trait—one that empowers us to navigate life's uncertainties with grit and grace.

Learning and Growth from Setbacks

Every setback holds the potential for insight. Reflecting on difficulties reveals areas where we can mature emotionally, spiritually, and mentally. These moments often develop patience, humility, and resourcefulness—traits not easily cultivated in ease. Setbacks also help us discover hidden strengths, clarify priorities, and appreciate progress. When we view challenges as lessons rather than losses, we transform failure into wisdom and become better equipped for future decisions.

Embracing Failure as Part of the Journey

Failure can feel like the end, but it's often the beginning of real growth. Embracing failure means removing the stigma around mistakes and recognizing their role in progress. When we release the fear of imperfection, we take creative risks, innovate, and stretch beyond our limits. Failure teaches resilience, flexibility, and determination. When we treat failure as a teacher—not a verdict—we step into a mindset that values growth over perfection and movement over stagnation.

Developing Patience and Endurance

True growth requires time. Challenges test our patience and demand endurance, especially when progress feels slow or invisible. Patience teaches us to wait with hope, to persevere when outcomes are uncertain, and to trust that growth is unfolding even when we don't see it. Endurance builds strength—not just physically, but emotionally and spiritually—allowing us to stay the course despite fatigue or discouragement. Together, patience and endurance remind us that lasting growth isn't rushed—it's cultivated.

Adapting and Learning Flexibility

Flexibility is essential when life doesn't go as planned. Challenges often force us to release control, reassess our path, and try new approaches. Flexibility allows us to adapt without giving up—to bend without breaking. It fosters creativity, openness, and humility, helping us respond to change with curiosity instead of fear. In a fast-changing world, flexibility is a strength that enables us to remain steady without becoming rigid, and responsive without becoming reactive.

Encouraging Others Through Our Example

Our response to difficulty has the power to encourage those around us. When we face hardship with grace, perseverance, and humility, we become living examples of resilience and hope. Others notice. Whether it's our children, colleagues, friends, or community, people are influenced by how we navigate trials. By embracing challenges with strength and optimism, we show others what is possible and offer silent encouragement that they, too, can overcome.

Living a Life of Purpose Through Growth

A meaningful life isn't one without struggle—it's one shaped through it. Challenges refine our character, strengthen our faith, and bring clarity to our calling. Each trial builds the foundation for greater wisdom, empathy, and courage. When we view life's hardships as chapters in a larger story of purpose, we see how growth and struggle are deeply intertwined. Embracing this truth allows us to live intentionally, leaving behind a legacy of resilience, maturity, and hope.

Choosing to see obstacles as opportunities is a powerful shift that impacts our own lives and those of others. By facing difficulty with perseverance, patience, and grace, we create a legacy not of avoidance, but of transformation. Those who watch us—especially younger generations—learn that adversity does not define us; our response does. This perspective shapes lives, families, and communities, proving that even the hardest seasons can yield the deepest growth.

Focusing on Eternal Rather Than Temporal Things

Choosing to prioritize what truly lasts over what is temporary can transform how we approach life. In a world that often values wealth, status, and material success, Scripture calls us to focus on what is eternal—our relationship with God, our character, and the legacy of love and service we leave behind. When we shift our focus from fleeting rewards to lasting significance, we find purpose beyond the moment and peace that surpasses understanding.

Looking for God's Will

The first step in focusing on eternal things is to seek God's will in every area of life. Through prayer, Scripture, and listening to the Holy Spirit, we align our desires with God's purpose. This daily practice keeps our focus steady and our intentions pure. When our goals reflect God's love and wisdom, we begin to live with deeper meaning, free from the distractions of worldly pursuits.

Loving God and Loving others

Jesus said the greatest commandments are to love God with all our heart, soul, and mind, and to love our neighbor as ourselves. When we anchor our lives in these truths, we shift from self-centered living to others-focused purpose. Acts of love, compassion, forgiveness, and service become our legacy. These are eternal investments—ways of living that outlast possessions or achievements and echo into the lives of others long after we're gone.

Helping Others Reflectively in Faith

Serving others is one of the most practical ways to invest in eternal things. Jesus taught that greatness is found not in being served, but in serving. Each time we give of ourselves—whether through time, prayer, encouragement, or resources—we shape lives and deepen our connection to what matters most. Service humbles us and reminds us that people are more valuable than possessions, and kindness is more impactful than recognition.

Storing Up Treasures in Heaven

In Matthew 6:19–20, Jesus warns against storing treasures on earth, where moth and rust destroy, and thieves break in and steal. Instead, He urges us to store up treasures in heaven—acts of faith, integrity, and compassion that reflect God's heart. These treasures cannot be measured in dollars or possessions, but they are priceless in the eyes of God. They shape our souls and leave a spiritual inheritance that no circumstance can diminish.

Focusing on the Kingdom of God

Prioritizing the Kingdom of God gives our lives eternal focus. When we seek His Kingdom first, as Matthew 6:33 teaches, everything else falls into place. This mindset helps us make decisions based on eternal values—truth, grace, love—rather than worldly rewards. It grounds us in faith and gives our actions lasting significance. Living with this focus doesn't mean we abandon daily responsibilities; it means we carry them out with divine purpose and perspective.

When we live for the eternal, we discover fulfillment that temporary success can never provide. We find joy not in accumulation, but in giving. We find peace not in control, but in surrender. We build a life that reflects God's heart and points others toward His goodness. And in doing so, we craft a legacy not defined by what we had—but by how we loved, served, and lived with purpose.

Focusing on eternal rather than temporal things helps us rise above the noise of the world. It clarifies our values, fuels our decisions, and shapes a legacy that outlives us. When we live with this perspective, we experience life more deeply, love more fully, and lead others toward lasting hope. It is a reminder that our time is brief—but our impact can be eternal.

IMPORTANCE OF 5 PURPOSEFUL LIVING

Importance of Helping Others

Developing a Sense of Purpose

Helping others directs our lives as we shift our focus from self-centered goals to those that benefit the community. This outward focus aligns our lives with meaningful purpose, reminding us that true fulfillment often comes from making a difference in someone else's life. By contributing

Helping others fosters empathy, patience, and selflessness—qualities vital for personal growth.

positively to others, we deepen our understanding of purposeful living, creating value that extends beyond ourselves.

Building Stronger Communities

When we help those around us, we strengthen the links within our communities. Acts of service develop trust and solidarity, helping to build a supportive environment where everyone feels valued. Ecclesiastes 4:9-10 explains this beautifully: *"Two are better than one... If either of them falls, one can help the other up."* This idea of reciprocal support encourages us to perceive community as a network of shared care and connection.

Enhancing Personal Growth and Empathy

Helping others fosters empathy, patience, and selflessness—qualities vital for personal growth. Understanding others' struggles makes us more compassionate, establishing attributes that enrich our lives and relationships. Philippians 2:4 encapsulates this idea: *"Let each of you look not only to his own interests but also to the interests of others."* By valuing empathy, we grow as individuals and deepen our relationships.

Creating a Ripple Effect of Kindness

One act of kindness can inspire others to act similarly, generating a positive ripple effect. This impact multiplies each modest gesture, establishing a culture of compassion. Hebrews 10:24 urges us, *"And let us consider how we may spur one another on toward love and good deeds."* Our actions may motivate people to join this cycle of kindness and mutual support.

Building a Sense of Gratitude and Perspective

Helping others encourages us to appreciate our own circumstances, generating gratitude. Witnessing others' resilience can transform our perspective, allowing us to view our lives with deeper respect. This emotion of appreciation enhances our joy as we acknowledge our blessings and recognize the importance of supporting those around us.

Fostering Spiritual and Moral Fulfillment

Helping others aligns us with spiritual and moral principles that emphasize compassion and charity. By serving others, we fulfill Jesus 'command in Matthew 25:40: *"Truly I tell you, whatever you did for one of the least of these brothers and sisters of mine, you did for me."* In assisting others, we strengthen our relationship with God and live purposefully and faithfully.

Leaving a Legacy of Compassion

A life of service builds a legacy remembered not for wealth or rank but for kindness and compassion. Proverbs 22:1 reminds us, *"A good name is more desirable than great riches; to be esteemed is better than silver or gold."* Through acts of kindness, we leave behind a legacy that inspires future generations to value empathy and service, passing on a message of love and purpose.

The Role of Purposeful Living in Our Lives

Providing Direction and Clarity

Purposeful living offers a clear direction that simplifies decision-making and prioritization. When we have a strong sense of purpose, we're better equipped to decide which paths align with our values and goals. This direction serves as a compass, guiding us away from distractions and helping us focus on actions that truly contribute to our long-term fulfillment. For instance, if someone's purpose involves positively impacting the environment, they might prioritize sustainable practices and avoid industries or activities that harm nature. Knowing our purpose saves time and energy on unimportant matters, making our lives more productive and intentional. This clarity reduces feelings of confusion or aimlessness, replacing them with a focused approach that brings order and fulfillment to our daily lives.

Enhancing Resilience and Strength

Purposeful living strengthens our resilience, especially when life becomes challenging. Purpose serves as an anchor, reminding us of the deeper meaning behind our actions and helping us endure temporary hardships. When faced with setbacks, a clear sense of purpose helps us stay committed instead of becoming discouraged. For example, someone devoted to helping their community might encounter obstacles, but their purpose motivates them to persist, understanding the significance of their work. Purpose gives us a reason to push through difficulties, reframing obstacles as part of the journey rather than reasons to give up. This resilience is essential for personal growth, enabling us to emerge from tough situations stronger and better prepared to face future challenges.

Promoting Personal Growth and Fulfillment
Purposeful living encourages continual growth and development. When we are dedicated to a meaningful goal, we naturally seek opportunities to learn, expand our knowledge, and acquire new skills. This commitment to growth enhances our capabilities and deepens our understanding of ourselves. For example, someone called to work in healthcare might invest in training, communication, or empathy exercises to serve their purpose more effectively. This mindset promotes lifelong learning, as each step forward brings us closer to fulfilling our purpose. Such growth leads to a satisfying sense of accomplishment as we evolve in both skill and character. Each achievement, no matter how small, draws us nearer to a fully lived purpose, resulting in profound, lasting fulfillment.

Fostering Connection and Community
Living purposefully often involves a commitment to causes or actions that benefit others, resulting in deeper relationships and

a stronger sense of community. When we pursue goals that align with our purpose, we naturally connect with others who share similar values. For example, someone passionate about social justice may find solidarity among activists and advocates, forming bonds rooted in shared purpose and passion. Purposeful living often drives us to support others, creating a sense of belonging and mutual encouragement. These relationships amplify our impact, and through community, we contribute to something greater than ourselves. This collective connection enhances our lives, fuels our motivation, and affirms that we are part of a larger, meaningful mission.

Aligning with Spiritual and Moral Values

Purposeful living often reflects our spiritual and moral convictions, allowing us to live in harmony with the principles we cherish. For people of faith, purposeful living may mean fulfilling a higher calling or divine mission. Proverbs 19:21 reinforces this truth: *"Many are the plans in a person's heart, but the Lord's purpose prevails."* Aligning our actions with our beliefs brings inner peace and spiritual fulfillment, as we devote ourselves to something larger than ourselves. For instance, someone who feels called to serve others might volunteer, donate, or work in professions that support the well-being of others. Living according to our core values strengthens our integrity and deepens our spiritual life, as each choice becomes an expression of what we believe to be right and just.

Creating a Legacy of Meaning and Impact

Living with purpose defines the legacy we leave behind. When we dedicate ourselves to meaningful goals and make a positive impact on others, our influence extends beyond our own lifetime. A purposeful life includes actions marked by kindness, integrity, and a desire to better the world—whether through personal relationships, professional efforts, or community involvement. Such a legacy serves as a powerful example for others to follow. For example, a teacher who inspires generations of students leaves an imprint that extends far into the future. Purposeful living is remembered not only for what was accomplished but for the goodness it cultivated, encouraging others to build lives that matter.

Bringing Joy and Contentment

Purposeful living fosters a joy and contentment that transcends temporary pleasures. When our lives are aligned with meaning, we experience deep satisfaction, knowing we're contributing positively to the world. This fulfillment endures, forming a lasting foundation of joy that isn't dependent on external factors. For example, someone committed to uplifting others may feel immense joy in witnessing the lives improved by their actions—

creating happiness grounded not in personal gain, but in meaningful service. Purposeful living infuses each day with significance, even transforming routine tasks into valuable contributions. As we align our daily efforts with our deeper mission, we find a sustained sense of joy and satisfaction rooted in knowing our lives truly matter.

Cultivating a Spirit of Generosity

The Biblical Foundation of Generosity

The Bible offers abundant guidance on the importance of generosity, portraying it not only as a virtue but as a vital expression of faith and purposeful living. Proverbs 11:24 captures this paradoxically powerful truth: *"One person gives freely, yet gains even more; another withholds unduly but comes to poverty."* This verse emphasizes that open-handed giving leads to greater blessing, while hoarding leads to spiritual emptiness. Scripture consistently presents generosity as an act of trust in God's provision—a practice that reflects the heart of God and draws us into deeper relationship with Him.

In the Bible, generosity encompasses far more than financial giving; it includes sharing time, talents, love, and compassion. Jesus consistently emphasized this holistic generosity, teaching that true wealth is measured not by accumulation but by our willingness to share. In Acts 20:35, Paul quotes Jesus: "It is more blessed to give than to receive." This reveals the joy that comes not from what we acquire, but from the blessings we bestow upon others. Giving becomes a sacred act—an extension of our faith that brings us closer to God.

Biblical teachings also urge us to give without fanfare or desire for recognition. In Matthew 6:3-4, Jesus instructs: "But when you give to the needy, do not let your left hand know what your right hand is doing, so that your giving may be in secret. Then your Father, who sees what is done in secret, will reward you." This reminds us that true generosity comes from a place of humility, not performance. It's the quiet, unseen acts of love that carry the greatest spiritual reward.

Generosity is ultimately a reflection of God's character. As recipients of His grace, love, and provision, we are called to emulate His generosity. 1 John 3:17-18 puts it plainly: *"If anyone has material possessions and sees a brother or sister in need but has no pity on them, how can the love of God be in that person? Dear children, let us not love with words or speech but with actions and in truth."* When we give, we become vessels of God's love—channels through which His compassion and care flow into the world.

Beyond simply addressing needs, generosity is a spiritual discipline that transforms us. Every act of giving is a step closer to

God, reaffirming our reliance on His provision rather than our possessions. Embracing the biblical call to generosity infuses our lives with purpose, draws us nearer to God, and enables us to reflect His grace in a self-centered world. Living generously becomes a sacred calling—a way to embody Christian love and fulfill our divine purpose.

The Personal Benefits of Generosity

Generosity brings blessing not only to the recipient but also to the giver, enriching the giver's life with deep fulfillment and a stronger sense of purpose. Proverbs 11:25 proclaims, *"A generous person will prosper; whoever refreshes others will be refreshed."* This reveals a profound truth: when we pour into others, we are replenished in return—emotionally, spiritually, and relationally. Giving strengthens our connections. In Luke 6:38, Jesus says, *"Give, and it will be given to you. A good measure, pressed down, shaken together and running over, will be poured into your lap. For with the measure you use, it will be measured to you."* Generosity, then, becomes a foundation for trust and reciprocity. As we give without expectation, we cultivate deeper relationships based on compassion, support, and mutual respect—relationships that endure and enrich our lives.

Generosity also leads to peace. Knowing we have made a positive difference in someone's life brings a deep, lasting sense of joy that far surpasses fleeting pleasure. Acts 20:35 reminds us: "It is more blessed to give than to receive." This blessing is not just spiritual—it manifests as emotional well-being, satisfaction, and peace of heart. Generosity becomes more than a kind gesture; it becomes a life-giving act that aligns us with divine purpose and nourishes our souls.

Developing a Generous Spirit
Cultivating generosity begins with a shift in mindset. We must first acknowledge that all we have—our time, talents, resources—are gifts from God, entrusted to us for the benefit of others. This understanding moves us from ownership to stewardship. As stewards, we recognize our role is not to hoard blessings but to distribute them with intentionality and love. When we live with open hands, we align ourselves with a greater purpose: extending God's goodness through every resource entrusted to us.

Generosity is not limited to wealth. Sharing your time to comfort someone, offering your talents to help another succeed, or simply being emotionally present are all acts of profound generosity. This holistic approach broadens our understanding of what it means to live generously, making it accessible to everyone, regardless of financial status. Every person has something valuable to give.

True generosity also requires sacrifice. It's about choosing to give even when it's uncomfortable or inconvenient. Jesus praised the widow in Luke 21:1-4 who gave two small coins—everything she had. Her offering, though small in amount, was rich in faith and love. This teaches us that the value of our generosity lies not in its size, but in its sincerity. Giving sacrificially invites us to put others 'needs before our own comfort, mirroring Christ's selfless love.

2 Corinthians 9:7 offers guidance: *"Each of you should give what you have decided in your heart to give, not reluctantly or under*

compulsion, for God loves a cheerful giver." This affirms that generosity should spring from a joyful heart, not a sense of guilt or duty. Giving cheerfully reflects trust in God's continued provision and transforms giving into worship—a grateful response to divine abundance.

As we grow in generosity, we grow closer to God. John 3:16 declares the ultimate act of divine generosity: *"For God so loved the world that he gave his one and only Son..."* When we give freely, we mirror God's heart, allowing His love to shape our lives. A generous spirit enhances our spiritual walk, enriches our purpose, and leaves behind a legacy of love and grace that blesses generations.

Generosity as an Expression of Purposeful Living
Living a life of purpose goes beyond personal success or material accumulation—it calls for a heart fully engaged in generosity, kindness, and selflessness. Purposeful living means recognizing that our lives are meant to have a meaningful impact on others, and one of the most powerful ways we do that is through giving. When we adopt a generous mindset, we begin to invest in eternal values rather than temporary gains. Every act of giving becomes a building block in a legacy that transcends our own lifespans.

In Matthew 6:19–20, Jesus offers clear wisdom: *"Do not store up for yourselves treasures on earth, where moths and vermin destroy, and where thieves break in and steal. But store up for yourselves treasures in heaven..."* This passage challenges us to reframe our priorities—not to focus on accumulating wealth or possessions, but to cultivate spiritual riches through generosity, compassion, and selfless love. These treasures in heaven—acts of kindness, moments of service, and sacrificial giving—cannot be lost or stolen. They endure beyond this life and ripple into eternity.

Generosity, then, becomes a visible manifestation of our inner purpose. When we give of our time, energy, and resources, we embody our commitment to something far greater than ourselves. A life that gives is a life that uplifts, supports, and heals. Purposeful living means allowing God's grace to flow through us into the lives of others. Proverbs 22:9 declares, *"The generous will themselves be blessed, for they share their food with the poor."* This blessing is not just material—it is spiritual, emotional, and deeply personal. When we give, we grow.

Living generously also draws us closer to the heart of God. His character is generous, and He invites us to mirror that trait in our daily lives. When we prioritize giving, we align ourselves with divine intention, reminding ourselves and others of the boundless compassion of our Creator. Each act of generosity is an act of worship—a declaration that we trust God's provision and choose to be vessels of His love.

By using what we have to serve others, we contribute to a greater purpose that breathes meaning into our actions. Even the smallest gesture can spark transformation. Generosity turns routine into revelation, converting the mundane into ministry. As we become more intentional with our giving, our lives begin to take on a shape that reflects eternity—defined not by what we have gained, but by how deeply we've loved and how freely we've given.

Through generosity, we construct a life that resonates with lasting value and spiritual richness. Our purpose becomes clear: to love, to serve, to give. And in doing so, we create a legacy not measured in accolades, but in lives touched, burdens lifted, and faith renewed. This is the essence of living purposefully—a daily devotion to giving in such a way that our lives point others toward God's grace.

Generosity doesn't just transform those we help; it transforms us. And as we continue to live with open hands and compassionate hearts, we participate in a divine cycle that blesses, uplifts, and endures.

Embracing Your Identity in Christ

Understanding Our Identity in Christ

Our identity in Christ is central to how we view ourselves, our purpose, and our relationship with God. When we place our faith in Jesus, we are reborn spiritually, becoming new creations. This transformation is profound, as 2 Corinthians 5:17 tells us: *"Therefore, if anyone is in Christ, he is a new creation. The old has passed away; behold, the new has come."* In Christ, we are no longer defined by our past mistakes, insecurities, or failures. Instead, our identity is rooted in Jesus 'sacrifice, His victory over sin, and the immense love God has for us as His children.

This new identity means that God sees us through the lens of grace and redemption, not through judgment or condemnation. We are called beloved, forgiven, and chosen—regardless of what the world says or how we view ourselves. Accepting this identity calls for a shift in perspective, where God's view becomes the defining truth about us. As children of God, we are invited to walk confidently in this truth, allowing it to shape our self-worth, our choices, and our purpose. Embracing our identity in Christ anchors us in something unshakable, empowering us to face life knowing we are deeply loved and eternally valued by our Creator.

Why Embracing Our Identity in Christ is Essential?
Understanding who we are in Christ is essential for living a purposeful life. When we embrace this identity, we live with spiritual confidence and emotional clarity. This confidence isn't rooted in our accomplishments but in our secure place in God's heart. We realize that we are fully accepted and valued—not because of what we do, but because of who we are in Him. This recognition guards us from the trap of seeking approval from others—be it through success, popularity, or possessions—which often leads to disappointment and insecurity.

Psalm 139:14 affirms this truth: *"I praise you because I am fearfully and wonderfully made; your works are wonderful, I know that full well."* When we accept that we were uniquely and purposefully created by God, we stop measuring our worth by worldly standards. Instead, we begin to understand that every gift, flaw, and experience plays a part in God's greater design. This understanding provides stability during life's storms, giving us the resilience to stay rooted in our divine purpose—even in the face of doubt, failure, or hardship.

Practical Steps to Embrace Our Identity in Christ

Living out our identity in Christ requires intentional practice. We must continually remind ourselves of who we are in God's eyes and train our minds to embrace that truth.

Reflect on Scripture: The Bible is rich with affirmations of our identity in Christ. Verses like John 1:12—*"Yet to all who did receive him, to those who believed in his name, he gave the right to become children of God"*—are powerful reminders. Meditating daily on these truths renews our minds, silences self-doubt, and grounds us in God's promises.

Stay in Prayer: Prayer strengthens our relationship with God and allows us to hear His voice concerning who we are. In moments of quiet prayer, we can ask God to reveal more about our purpose and identity. He delights in confirming His love for us and guiding us in our journey.

Engage in Worship: Worship shifts our focus from ourselves to God. It reminds us of His majesty and our place as His beloved. During worship, we often experience a realignment of perspective, seeing ourselves as God sees us—loved, chosen, and purposeful.

Find Community: Spiritual growth thrives in community. Surrounding ourselves with other believers who affirm our identity in Christ helps us stay grounded. Fellowship strengthens our sense of belonging, offers accountability, and reinforces that we're part of something greater than ourselves.

Serve Others: Jesus showed us that love in action reflects our identity. When we serve others, we embody Christ's love, demonstrating humility, compassion, and selflessness. Service reminds us of our calling and connects us more deeply to God's heart and mission.

Living Boldly and Confidently in Our Identity
Embracing our identity in Christ gives us the courage to live boldly, no matter our circumstances. Our assurance isn't dependent on external success but grounded in God's unwavering love. Romans 8:38-39 powerfully affirms this: *"For I am convinced that neither death nor life... nor anything else in all creation will be able to separate us from the love of God that is in Christ Jesus our Lord."* This truth fortifies us to step into difficult situations, take

risks for God's kingdom, and persevere through hardship, knowing we are never alone.

Living confidently in Christ also involves extending grace to ourselves. It means letting go of past failures, embracing God's forgiveness, and moving forward without shame. When we understand that we are made new in Christ, we can release guilt and fear, opening our lives to new opportunities and joy. This freedom enables us to live with intention, fulfilling our God-given purpose.

Overcoming the Pressures of the World Through Our Identity in Christ

The world often pressures us to conform to its ever-changing standards—seeking approval through appearance, status, material wealth, and popularity. These expectations can be exhausting and lead us to measure our worth by temporary, shallow metrics. However, our identity in Christ liberates us from these worldly demands. It reminds us that we are set apart and called to live by a higher, eternal standard.

Romans 12:2 urges believers with a powerful directive: *"Do not conform to the pattern of this world, but be transformed by the renewing of your mind. Then you will be able to test and approve what God's will is—his good, pleasing and perfect will."* This transformation begins internally. By renewing our minds with God's truth, we gain clarity and spiritual strength to resist external pressures and stay aligned with His purpose.

Living out our identity in Christ means we are no longer swayed by trends or dependent on the approval of others to feel valuable. Our value is rooted in something infinitely greater—God's unchanging love and the divine calling He has placed on our lives. This truth empowers us to be secure in who we are, regardless of society's opinions or rejections. It gives us the courage to stand firm in our convictions, even when they contradict popular culture.

By embracing our God-given identity, we learn to live with integrity, peace, and unwavering purpose. Our identity in Christ becomes a shield—guarding us from insecurity and compromise. We can walk through a world that demands conformity and still remain true to who God says we are. This spiritual clarity enables us to live with intentionality, investing our time and energy into what matters most: loving God, serving others, and glorifying Him with our lives.

Encouraging and Uplifting Others

Encouraging and uplifting others is fundamental to living a purposeful life that aligns with God's teachings. In a world where so many struggle with loneliness, fear, and self-doubt, encouragement becomes a powerful tool for spreading hope and strengthening those around us. This encouragement not only uplifts the person receiving it but also deeply blesses the encourager, bringing a shared sense of joy and purpose. Biblical encouragement goes beyond simple compliments or praise; it involves inspiring others to live faithfully, love boldly, and pursue God's calling. By prioritizing encouragement, we become God's instruments of love, joy, and comfort, helping others rise to their potential and find strength in Him.

The Bible calls us to encourage one another frequently, reminding us of our responsibility to be a source of strength and positivity. 1 Thessalonians 5:11 says, *"Therefore encourage one another and build each other up, just as you are doing."* This verse highlights how encouragement is an ongoing practice that requires intentionality, and a heart centered on compassion. When we make it a part of our daily lives to build others up, we reflect the love of God and reinforce our sense of purpose, showing that life's true worth lies in relationships grounded in love and faith..

The Importance of Community and Gathering Together
Encouragement is most powerful when experienced in the context of community. Being part of a Christian community provides a space where individuals can both receive and extend support, sharing their joys and sorrows. Hebrews 10:24-25 underscores the value of gathering together: *"And let us consider how we may spur one another on toward love and good deeds, not giving up meeting together, as some are in the habit of doing, but encouraging one another—and all the more as you see the Day approaching."* This verse reminds us that gathering as believers is more than tradition; it is a spiritual necessity that fosters growth and mutual encouragement.

Gathering in community allows us to uplift one another in ways that would be difficult in isolation. Sharing our struggles and victories helps us recognize that we are not alone in our journey. In moments of adversity, the presence of a caring community provides strength we might not otherwise access. When one member is down, others step in to lift them up, reinforcing a network of love, resilience, and shared faith. Within this environment, encouragement becomes a gift in constant circulation—each person contributing to and benefiting from the strength of the whole. By choosing to gather regularly and engage meaningfully, we cultivate a culture of encouragement that supports us through life's trials and triumphs.

The Power of Kind and Gracious Words

Words are incredibly powerful—they can inspire, heal, and motivate, or they can harm and discourage. Proverbs 16:24 beautifully illustrates this truth: *"Gracious words are a honeycomb, sweet to the soul and healing to the bones."* This verse highlights that words can reach deep within a person, offering sweetness to the soul and healing to wounded spirits. When we speak words of encouragement, we bring life, hope, and comfort to others, reinforcing their faith and affirming their worth.

Encouraging remarks don't need to be elaborate. Often, the simplest expressions carry the greatest depth. For someone experiencing a difficult moment, a few sincere words of affirmation or a reminder of God's promises can ignite hope and confidence. This is why it's essential to be intentional with our speech—our words carry lasting impact and have the potential to either build someone up or tear them down. In times when we know someone is struggling, even one word of encouragement may be the very thing that helps them continue. We can remind them of God's unfailing love, the strength He provides, and the assurance that they are never alone. By choosing our words carefully and purposefully, we transform everyday conversations into opportunities to extend grace and encouragement, reflecting God's heart through our interactions.

Using Barnabas as an Example: A Life of Encouragement

The Bible offers many examples of encouragement, but one of the most inspiring is the life of Barnabas. Known as the "Son of Encouragement," Barnabas exemplified a life dedicated to uplifting others and advancing God's mission. Acts 4:36–37 introduces him as *"Joseph, a Levite from Cyprus, whom the apostles called Barnabas (which means 'son of encouragement'), sold a field he owned and brought the money and placed it at the apostles' feet."* This act of generosity demonstrates how Barnabas went beyond words—he provided tangible support to empower the early church. His willingness to make personal sacrifices for the sake of God's kingdom reveals how practical and impactful encouragement can be.

Barnabas played a pivotal role in the early church, and his support for others had lasting impact. When Paul first converted to Christianity, many believers were hesitant to accept him due to his past persecution of Christians. But Barnabas saw Paul's transformation and potential. Acts 9:27 recounts how Barnabas took Paul to the apostles and vouched for him, helping Paul gain acceptance and begin his ministry. Barnabas's encouragement legitimized Paul's calling and opened doors that might have otherwise remained closed. His faith in Paul helped shape one of the greatest apostles in Christian history. This powerful story demonstrates how believing in someone can radically change their life. Following Barnabas's example, we too can help others walk boldly in their purpose, often unlocking potential they may not yet see in themselves.

Practical Ways to Encourage and Uplift Others

Encouragement can be woven into the fabric of our everyday lives through simple, consistent actions. It doesn't require a platform or grand gestures—just a willing heart and intentionality. Here are several ways to make encouragement part of your daily walk:

Seek Out Opportunities: Developing a spirit of encouragement starts with being attentive to the people around us. Look for those who may need a word of hope or a supportive presence. It could be as simple as checking in on a quiet coworker, writing a heartfelt message to a struggling friend, or reaching out to someone walking through a season of loss or uncertainty. Encouragement is most impactful when it's proactive and personal. When we open our eyes to the needs of others, we often discover opportunities to uplift them that we would have otherwise overlooked.

Mind Your Words: Words carry weight. Proverbs 18:21 reminds us, *"The tongue has the power of life and death."* This is a call to be mindful of how we speak. Our conversations should be infused with grace, kindness, and truth—whether we're speaking to family, colleagues, or strangers. Words of praise, affirmation, and empathy can transform a person's day, even their life. Encouragement doesn't require elaborate speeches. A simple "I believe in you" or "God has great plans for your life" can be enough to plant a seed of hope that blossoms in someone's spirit. Consistent, positive speech becomes a habit that uplifts everyone around us.

Encourage Through Actions: Sometimes, the most powerful encouragement comes through action. A warm gesture, a thoughtful gift, or helping someone without being asked speaks volumes. Just as Barnabas sold his possessions to meet the needs of the early church, we too can give generously—our time, energy, and resources—to support those around us. Actions validate our words and demonstrate a genuine care that resonates deeply. Whether it's bringing a meal to a neighbor, volunteering at church, or stepping in when someone is overwhelmed, our willingness to act reinforces our desire to uplift others.

Be Present and Listen: Encouragement isn't always about offering solutions. Sometimes, the greatest gift we can give is our presence. Listening without interrupting, judging, or immediately offering advice allows people to feel heard and valued. Many carry silent burdens and simply need someone to acknowledge their pain. Being fully present—putting aside distractions to engage with sincerity—shows people they matter. This kind of encouragement strengthens emotional bonds and fosters healing. It's a ministry of presence that requires humility, compassion, and intentional focus.

Pray for Others: Prayer is one of the most profound and powerful forms of encouragement. When we intercede on behalf of others, we invite God into their situations and declare our belief in His power to work in their lives. Sharing that we are praying for someone brings comfort and assurance that they are not facing their trials alone. Praying with someone in the moment—laying hands, speaking Scripture, or simply offering quiet support—can provide supernatural peace and strength. Through prayer, we lift others spiritually and point them to the ultimate source of hope and healing.

Living a Life of Encouragement

Encouragement is not merely a helpful act; it's a calling—one that reflects the heart of Christ and reveals the nature of purposeful living. Choosing to make encouragement a lifestyle transforms not only the lives of others but also our own. It becomes a rhythm of grace that beats through every word we speak, every action we take, and every relationship we build.

When we intentionally uplift those around us, we participate in a sacred mission. Each encouraging word plants seeds of hope; each supportive gesture becomes a bridge to healing. These small, consistent efforts create a ripple effect that stretches far beyond what we can see—impacting hearts, restoring confidence, and igniting purpose in others. Encouragement can change the course of someone's life in a moment, and that power is in our hands each day.

It also enriches our own spiritual walk. As we pour into others, we draw closer to God. Encouragement aligns us with His will: to love, serve, and reflect His goodness. In lifting others, we discover deeper joy, humility, and fulfillment. Our purpose becomes clearer as we live not just for ourselves, but as vessels of grace. Encouragement transforms ordinary moments into divine appointments, where our words and actions become instruments of God's peace and love.

Encouragement also leaves a lasting legacy. While wealth and success fade, the impact of a kind word or a compassionate heart endures. A life marked by encouragement becomes a testimony of God's love in action. It reminds people that they matter, that they're seen, and that they are not alone. In a world so often marked by criticism and fear, the encourager becomes a light—a beacon pointing others toward hope, healing, and the truth of God's promises.

By choosing to live this way, we reflect Christ. His ministry was filled with words of life, healing, forgiveness, and promise. He saw the overlooked, embraced the outcast, and spoke hope into the broken. As His followers, we're called to do the same. Our encouragement is not empty positivity—it is anchored in the truth of God's Word and fueled by His Spirit.

In embracing encouragement as a way of life, we become agents of change. We carry God's message of love in our voices and in our presence. We become builders—of faith, of courage, of community. Every word of kindness, every gesture of support, becomes a brick in the foundation of someone else's hope.

Let us then commit, daily, to this sacred purpose. Let us look for opportunities to encourage, to lift, to comfort, and to strengthen. Let our lives echo the compassion of Christ, creating a legacy not just of kind words, but of transformed lives. Through encouragement, we live out our purpose—faithfully, joyfully, and in step with the heart of God.

VALUE OF 6 PURPOSEFUL LIVING

The Value of being Kind to Others.

Kindness is one of those traits that can alter everything, yet it often feels like something we ignore in our results-driven existence. It may be an act of civility, something we perform when it's convenient. But the reality is that compassion can alter not just others—but ourselves.

Embracing a spirit of kindness shows the deep essence of our shared humanity.

I remember a moment when I was strolling across a crowded

street, headed to an appointment, buried in my thoughts. I had a lot on my mind, balancing deadlines and obligations. Just as I was ready to enter a café, I spotted an older man standing at the door, appearing bewildered. I almost walked past him, thinking he must be alright, but something stopped me. I turned back and offered to help.

His face lit up when I asked if he needed directions, and he explained that he had lost his way to a nearby hospital where he was supposed to visit his wife. I could see the worry in his eyes. I walked with him without hesitation, helping him find the correct street. When we parted ways, he thanked me profusely—but I could feel something shift in me, too: a deep sense of peace and joy I hadn't expected.

In that moment, I realized that kindness isn't just about helping others; it's about connecting with them in a way that transcends mere interaction. Kindness is a form of love in action.

The Bible tells us in Ephesians 4:32, *"Be kind and compassionate to one another, forgiving each other, just as in Christ God forgave you."* This verse shows that kindness is not just a nice thing to do—it's an essential part of how we are called to live. It is part of what makes us more like Christ, who repeatedly showed kindness to the broken, the lonely, and the marginalized.

Acts of kindness need not be elaborate or showy. In the quiet moments of our daily lives, the little gestures truly matter: a friendly smile exchanged with a stranger, the comfort of lending an ear to a friend, or the simple act of sharing a warm meal with someone who needs it. Each action, regardless of its size, holds significance. In the quiet moments of our lives, as we extend kindness to others, we unknowingly set in motion a series of events impacting hearts and souls in ways that often remain unseen.

Embracing a spirit of kindness shows the deep essence of our shared humanity. It's not merely about our gifts; it's about the transformations we undergo—the expansion of our hearts, the discovery of purpose, and the deep pleasure that comes from understanding we've brought a touch of light to someone else's life.

Kindness doesn't always come easily, especially when we are wrapped up in our own struggles. But when we choose to be kind—not out of obligation, but out of love and grace—we mirror the heart of God. Just like He has shown endless kindness to us, we are called to do the same for others.

Actionable Steps to Incorporate Kindness into Your Daily Life

Kindness doesn't need to be complicated. It's in the little things—the moments when you choose to step outside of your world and connect with someone else meaningfully.

Practice Random Acts of Kindness

Pay it Forward: At the coffee shop, consider paying for the order of the person behind you. It doesn't have to be a grand gesture; a small act can brighten someone's day.

Leave an Uplifting Note: Write a short note of encouragement and leave it on a colleague's desk or in a friend's mailbox. A simple

"You've got this" or "You're doing great" can be a powerful reminder of someone's worth.

Compliment Someone: Give a genuine compliment to a stranger or a friend something specific that shows you've noticed them. Compliments like "I love your energy" or "Your kindness shines through" make people feel seen and appreciated.

Show Empathy and Active Listening
Put Down Your Phone: When someone shares something with you, take a moment to put down your distractions. Please give them your full attention, listen without interrupting, and show you care by asking follow up questions or simply nodding to show you understand.

Validate Their Feelings: Sometimes, kindness isn't about solving someone's problem but acknowledging their emotions. Phrases like, "That sounds tough" or "I can't imagine what you're going through, but I'm here for you" go a long way in showing empathy.

Check in: Send a text or quickly call someone you know who might be struggling. The simple act of checking in can make a huge difference in someone's day.

Volunteer Your Time or Skills
Give Your Time: Look for local organizations, shelters, or food

banks that could use an extra set of hands. Even a few hours can profoundly impact others, and you'll walk away feeling good about contributing to your community.

Share Your Skills: Offer to tutor a child, mentor someone starting a new job, or help a neighbor with gardening. We all have unique talents and skills that can brighten someone's life. Volunteering your expertise can make someone's life a little easier.

Support Causes: If you can't physically volunteer, consider supporting organizations financially, donating clothing, or organizing charity events. Every bit helps, and even the smallest contribution matters.

Be Mindful of Your Words and Actions

Practice Patience: Whether you're stuck in traffic or standing in a long line, instead of letting frustration build, take a deep breath and choose patience. Sometimes, kindness is simply refraining from snapping at someone in a stressful situation.

Offer Help Without Being Asked: If you see someone struggling with groceries or trying to carry something heavy, offer to help. We often wait for people to ask, but offering assistance can be a profound act of kindness.

Smile: A smile costs nothing but can make someone feel seen and appreciated. Smiling at a cashier, a neighbor, or a passerby can brighten their day more than you might realize.

Be Kind to Yourself

Practice Self Compassion: Often, we are quick to be kind to others but forget to extend that same grace to ourselves. Take a moment each day to acknowledge your worth, forgive yourself for past mistakes, and celebrate your accomplishments, no matter how small.

Give Yourself Time to Rest: Kindness isn't just about what you do for others. It's also about what you do for yourself. Take breaks when needed, and don't feel guilty for giving yourself time to recharge.

Pursuing Excellence in All That You Do

Life often feels like a whirlwind, full of demands and distractions. But within the chaos, there's a powerful way to ground ourselves and live with true purpose: by pursuing excellence in everything we do. With its timeless wisdom, the Bible consistently calls us to live intentionally, not just going through the motions but striving for something greater. And that something is excellence not as a pursuit of perfection but as a commitment to always doing our best, regardless of the circumstances.

Excellence is a mindset, not a destination. It's not about reaching some unattainable standard but about giving our best effort in each moment, knowing that each act has meaning. Colossians 3:23 reminds us, *"Whatever you do, work heartily, as for the Lord and not for men."* This verse reveals an essential truth: our efforts matter to God no matter how small they seem. We honor Him and ourselves when we approach our work, relationships, and personal growth with excellence.

The Impact of Excellence

Pursuing excellence is more than just a personal goal; it's a ripple that touches everyone around us. When we pour energy into our work, relationships, and daily habits, we create a foundation of integrity and discipline. We don't always get it right, but we're committed to giving our best, even when things are hard. And this effort, this consistency, transforms us.

Think about someone you know who consistently does their best at whatever they do. It could be a colleague who always goes the extra mile or a friend who shows up even when it's inconvenient. Something is inspiring about those people. They don't have to be perfect, but they carry themselves with a sense of purpose, and that energy is contagious. Their pursuit of excellence lifts others, encouraging them to elevate their standards. Excellence, it turns out, isn't just about achieving something for ourselves—it's about elevating the world around us.

Consider a painter who labors over each brushstroke, not for fame or recognition, but simply because they care deeply about their craft. That artist may not be the most famous or recognized, but their dedication to excellence has a profound impact. Not only does it produce something beautiful, but it serves as a reminder to all of us: how we show up in the world matters. Excellence touches lives in ways we might never fully understand, but that doesn't make it any less powerful.

Examples of Excellence in Action

The Bible contains examples of individuals who embraced a life of excellence. Take the Apostle Paul, for instance. His journey was challenging. He faced imprisonment, persecution, and hardship at every turn. Yet, in Philippians 3:14, Paul writes, *"I press on toward the goal to win the prize for which God has called me heavenward in Christ Jesus."* He didn't stop despite the obstacles. He kept pushing forward, relentlessly pursuing his calling. His life wasn't about fame or accolades; it was about faithfulness. He gave his best because he knew his purpose was greater than any temporary struggle.

In more modern times, we can look at people like Maya Angelou, who pursued excellence as a writer, speaker, educator, and activist. Her works, like I Know Why the Caged Bird Sings, didn't just entertain; they challenged minds and sparked change. She exemplified excellence through dedication to her craft and commitment to truth. Maya didn't just "show up" to her work. She poured herself into it, giving everything she had to make a lasting impact on the world.

In the business world, we see people like Steve Jobs, whose relentless drive for excellence in product design and innovation changed how we interact with technology. Jobs didn't settle for "good enough" in any aspect of his work. He demanded excellence from himself, his team, and his company. Because of this, he didn't just build a successful business—he reshaped an entire industry. The common thread in all these examples is that excellence isn't just about individual success. It's about making a difference. Excellence is a form of service to others. Whether you're an artist, an entrepreneur, or a teacher, your commitment to excellence can have a lasting impact on the people around you.

Practical Steps for Pursuing Excellence

How can we practically apply this principle of excellence to our lives? It's not something that happens overnight; it's a process and a daily commitment.

Set High Standards: It's easy to fall into the trap of doing just enough to get by. But excellence requires setting a higher bar. Ask yourself: What would it look like for me to give my best in this situation? Whether in your work, relationships, or personal development, strive to do more than meet the minimum.

Challenge yourself to exceed expectations—not for the sake of praise, but because you know that giving your best is a reflection of your values.

Cultivate Discipline: Excellence doesn't come without hard work. It requires discipline and consistency. If you want to achieve excellence in any area of life, you must put in the time and effort, even when it's inconvenient. This could mean waking up earlier to focus on your goals, committing yourself to daily practice, or simply showing up with a positive attitude, even when the work feels heavy.

Seek Continuous Improvement: The path to excellence is never truly complete. There's always room to grow, to learn, and to evolve. Romans 12:2 says, *"Do not conform to the pattern of this world, but be transformed by the renewing of your mind."* Pursuing excellence is a lifelong journey of personal growth and continuous learning. No matter how skilled or accomplished you become, there is always more to learn. Embrace that journey, and keep moving forward with humility and curiosity.

Do Everything for God's Glory: Everything shifts when we frame our work and efforts within the context of serving God. Our motivation is no longer just about personal success or approval. It's about honoring God with the talents He's given us.

Approaching our work with that mindset transforms mundane tasks into acts of worship. We find fulfillment not in recognition but in knowing that our efforts are pleasing to Him.

The Value of Taking in Strangers

Opening our hearts and homes to strangers is one of the most powerful ways to connect with others. It's not just about offering a place to stay or a meal but about showing kindness, trust, and humanity. In a world that can often feel fractured and disconnected, welcoming the stranger is an invitation to create bonds, foster understanding, and build a community that transcends borders, differences, and misunderstandings.

A Biblical Story of Hospitality

We can turn to a well-known biblical story that illustrates hospitality's profound impact to better understand the importance of welcoming strangers. The story is found in Genesis, chapter 18. Abraham, the patriarch of the Israelites, was sitting outside his tent when three strangers appeared. He did not recognize them, yet his response was immediate and filled with hospitality.

Genesis 18:2–3 says: *"Abraham looked up and saw three men standing nearby. When he saw them, he hurried from the entrance of his tent to meet them and bowed low to the ground. He said, 'If I have found favor in your eyes, my lord, do not pass your servant by.'"*

Abraham didn't hesitate. He invited these strangers to rest, wash their feet, and share a meal. He offered them the best of what he had—giving them the finest bread, meat, and curds. His willingness to care for them this way was not merely an act of kindness but a demonstration of his faith and belief in the sacred nature of hospitality. Abraham treated these visitors as royalty, although he had no idea they were angels sent by God.

After partaking in the meal, the visitors revealed their divine purpose: to deliver a message from God. They informed Abraham that his wife, Sarah, would bear a son despite her age. This son, Isaac, would become the father of the nation that would carry God's promise.

This story underscores a key principle: in welcoming strangers, we may unknowingly participate in something far greater than we can see. Abraham's hospitality wasn't just a gesture of kindness—it was a divine encounter crucial to fulfilling God's plan. His kindness to these visitors opened the door to blessings he could never have anticipated.

Historical and Cultural Examples of Hospitality

Historically, taking in strangers has been deeply ingrained in various cultures and traditions. Hospitality was once considered not just a social nicety but a sacred responsibility. In ancient Greece, the practice of xenia (guest-friendship) was more than politeness; it was a divine obligation. Strangers were often viewed as potential gods or messengers in disguise, and to deny them hospitality was believed to invite the wrath of the gods.

This tradition is reflected in the story of the Greek hero Odysseus, who was often shown hospitality during his long journey home. The gods themselves were believed to observe how strangers were treated. Hospitality, in this sense, became a means of connecting with the divine.

The Bible repeatedly emphasizes the importance of welcoming strangers. In the Old Testament, Leviticus 19:34 commands: *"The foreigner residing among you must be treated as your native-born. Love them as yourself, for you were foreigners in Egypt. I am the Lord your God."*

This passage directly explains why we should welcome strangers: we were once strangers ourselves. Our history includes times of displacement, fear, and the need for compassion from others. Similarly, in the New Testament, Hebrews 13:2 urges believers: *"Do not forget to show hospitality to strangers, for by so doing some people have shown hospitality to angels without knowing it."* Here, the Bible reinforces that opening our hearts to others—especially those we don't know—is not just noble. It's a way of participating in God's greater plan.

The Spiritual Perspective

The act of taking in strangers is deeply spiritual. In many religious traditions, hospitality is seen not just as a moral duty but as a reflection of one's faith. In Christianity, welcoming strangers is a direct command from Jesus Himself. In Matthew 25:35, Jesus says, *"For I was hungry and you gave me something to eat, I was thirsty and you gave me something to drink, I was a stranger and you invited me in."*

This passage highlights the profound spiritual significance of hospitality. When we invite the stranger into our lives, we are welcoming Christ Himself.

The Bible goes even further in Matthew 25:40, where Jesus says, *"Truly I tell you, whatever you did for one of the least of these brothers and sisters of mine, you did for me."*

By showing kindness and hospitality to those in need, we are not merely helping others—we are serving Christ. This teaching elevates the act of hospitality from a simple social gesture to a divine calling.

In Islam, hospitality is equally sacred. The Prophet Muhammad (peace be upon him) said, *"He who believes in Allah and the Last Day should honor his guest."*

This instruction emphasizes the importance of showing respect and kindness to those who are new, unfamiliar, or in need. It underscores that hospitality reflects one's faith and is an opportunity to demonstrate love for God's creation.

Similarly, Buddhism teaches that compassion should extend to all beings, including strangers. The Dalai Lama often speaks about the importance of seeing others as interconnected, reminding us that showing kindness to one person benefits the whole. When we extend hospitality to strangers, we are not just helping that person—we are contributing to the collective well-being of humanity.

Practical Ways to Welcome Strangers

The beauty of welcoming strangers is that it doesn't always require grand gestures. Some of the most meaningful acts of hospitality are simple and every day.

Here are a few practical ways you can welcome strangers into your life:

Be Present: Sometimes, the greatest gift we can offer is our attention. Take a moment to greet a new neighbor, ask someone how their day is going, or smile at a passerby. Small gestures like this can make a big difference in someone's life.

Extend a Hand of Friendship: If you notice someone new in your workplace, neighborhood, or church, take the initiative to invite them to lunch or coffee. It could be as simple as offering to show them around the area or providing information that might help them feel more at home.

Volunteer: Many organizations serve the needs of refugees, immigrants, or homeless individuals. Volunteering your time—even in small ways—can be an incredibly powerful way to help others feel welcome. Whether at a shelter, a community center, or a food bank, giving your time can help you connect with others while making a tangible difference in their lives.

Open Your Home: If you're able, consider opening your home to someone new to the area. A friend or family member may have a guest visiting from out of town, or perhaps someone needs temporary shelter. Even offering a spare room or a place on your couch can be a life-changing act of kindness.

Support Newcomers in Your Community: If a newcomer to your community is a refugee, a student, or a single parent, take time to support them. Help them learn about local resources, introduce them to people, or spend time getting to know them.

Pursuing Meaningful Relationships with God and Others

In life, we all crave connection—a deeper sense of meaning and fulfillment that transcends the routine of daily existence. One of the most powerful ways to live purposefully is through our relationships—not just with others but with God. These relationships shape who we are, how we view the world, and how we navigate our journey.

The Importance of a Relationship with God

Imagine walking through life with a constant companion who knows your heart, understands your struggles, and offers guidance when you feel lost. That is the relationship we can have with God. The Bible reminds us that we were created for a relationship with our Creator. In John 17:3, Jesus defines eternal life not as a distant, future promise but as something that begins with knowing God: *"Now this is eternal life: that they know you, the only true God, and Jesus Christ, whom you have sent."* This verse reveals that a deep connection with God is the foundation of true fulfillment.

When we cultivate a relationship with God, it becomes the wellspring of peace and purpose. Life's uncertainties don't seem as daunting when we know we are held in the hands of a loving Father. Trusting Him, surrendering to His will, and seeking His presence in daily moments give our lives clarity and direction.

In my own life, I've found that prayer isn't just about asking for help. It's about building trust. It's about learning that even in silence, God is present, guiding us with gentle nudges and speaking to us through His Word. And while God's direction may not always come with immediate answers, the relationship gives us the courage to move forward, even in uncertainty. This trust and peace form the cornerstone of purposeful living.

The Importance of Relationships with Others

Our connection with others plays an equally significant role in living with purpose. In Matthew 22:37-39, Jesus gave us a commandment that sums up the heart of our relationships: *"Love the Lord your God with all your heart, soul, and mind. This is the first and greatest commandment. And the second is like it: Love your neighbor as yourself."* Loving God and loving others are inseparable. You cannot claim to love God fully without extending that love to those around you.

Relationships with others are where we experience the joys of shared humanity. These connections—built on trust, respect, and love—nourish our hearts and help us grow. When we share our lives with others, we learn about them and ourselves. We see our flaws and strengths reflected in them. We learn patience, empathy, and forgiveness. We become better versions of ourselves through our efforts and how we enrich one another's lives.

Take, for example, the friendships that stand the test of time. These aren't casual acquaintances, but bonds formed through mutual understanding, support, and trust. True friendship means being there for each other, even when it's difficult. It's about lifting someone when they're down and being a source of encouragement when they feel weak. This kind of love is the fabric that weaves us together, creating a life full of meaning and connection.

Putting It into Practice

First, prioritize your relationship with God. Set aside time daily to pray, read Scripture, and reflect on His goodness. These moments allow you to reconnect with the source of your purpose and recalibrate your heart. As you grow in your relationship with God, His love will shape how you see the world and the people around you.

Second, invest in your relationships with others. Real, lasting relationships require time and effort. Whether it's a family member, friend, or neighbor, choose to show up. Listen with empathy, engage with care, and be present in the moments that matter. Practice forgiveness, because no relationship is without conflict. The goal isn't perfection but growth and reconciliation.

Lastly, serve others through your relationships. It's easy to focus on what you can gain, but true fulfillment comes when you give. Use your time, talents, and resources to lift others. Whether volunteering, supporting a cause, or simply showing kindness to someone in need, your actions will speak louder than words. You can't love others fully without being willing to serve them.

Ecclesiastes 4:9–10 offers this wisdom: *"Two are better than one, because they have a good return for their labor: If either of them falls, one can help the other up."* Life was never meant to be lived alone. By nurturing our relationship with God and with others, we find purpose and create a community of support that strengthens us all.

Ultimately, a purposeful life is rooted in relationships—first with God, and then with those He places around us. By intentionally investing in these relationships, we are not just living for ourselves but for something greater, something eternal.

SIGNIFICANCE OF 7 PURPOSEFUL LIVING

Purposeful living is about more than just existing—it's about embracing life with intention. It's about making a daily choice to live in a way that reflects our values, uplifts others, and leads to personal growth. This chapter explores the essential aspects of purposeful living: compassion, generosity, love, and service. These values are crucial for enriching our own lives and making a lasting impact on the world around us.

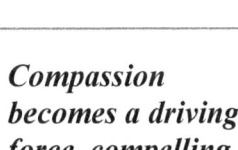

Compassion becomes a driving force, compelling us to meet the needs of others and make a difference in their lives.

The Role of Compassion in Purposeful Living

Compassion is more than just sympathy for someone else's suffering. It is a powerful force that drives us to act and improve the world by extending kindness and understanding to others. In the context of purposeful living, compassion is an essential ingredient. It gives our lives direction and meaning, aligning our actions with a deeper sense of responsibility toward the well-being of others.

Compassion as the Heart of Purposeful Living

At its core, compassion is the recognition of human vulnerability and suffering, combined with the desire to alleviate it. But it goes beyond simply feeling pity for someone; it compels us to step into the lives of others and offer help however we can. This could be through a listening ear, providing resources, or simply being present in someone's pain. Compassion connects us and shapes how we live out our purpose.

In Matthew 9:36, Jesus looks at the crowds with compassion: *"When He saw the crowds, He had compassion on them, because they were harassed and helpless, like sheep without a shepherd."* Jesus' compassion wasn't just an emotional reaction—it moved Him to act. He healed the sick, fed the hungry, and guided the lost. Compassion becomes a driving force, compelling us to meet the needs of others and make a difference in their lives.

The Power of Compassion to Transform Lives

I've had the privilege of witnessing firsthand how compassion transforms both the giver and the receiver. A few years ago, I was involved in a community outreach project to support families in crisis. One particular family stood out: an elderly couple living in poor conditions, struggling with health issues and financial difficulties. The first time I visited, the wife sat frail and exhausted in a dimly lit room. As we sat and talked, it became clear how deeply her circumstances had worn her down. But as we spent more time together—offering resources, providing meals, and simply listening to their stories—I saw a remarkable change. The couple started to believe that things could get better. Their outlook changed, not because of any material gift, but because they felt seen and cared for.

This experience taught me that compassion has the power to restore dignity. Sometimes, it's not about solving every problem, but about showing someone they are worthy of care, attention, and respect. Compassion allows us to make those connections, to step into someone else's world, even if just for a moment, and to offer them hope.

Biblical Insight

The Bible offers numerous examples of compassion in action, often illustrating how God's people are called to live with hearts full of mercy for others. In Colossians 3:12, Paul writes, *"Therefore, as God's chosen people, holy and dearly loved, clothe yourselves with compassion, kindness, humility, gentleness, and patience."* This verse urges us to "clothe ourselves" in compassion, making it an outward expression of our inner character. Just as we dress in clothes daily, compassion should be something we wear constantly—a part of who we are.

Jesus' ministry is a beautiful example of this. In Mark 6:34, when Jesus saw a large crowd gathered around Him, He was moved with compassion because they were like sheep without a shepherd. Rather than turn them away, He chose to teach them, care for them, and meet their needs. He showed us that compassion often requires action—it's not enough to feel for people; we must take steps to help them.

Compassion as a Source of Fulfillment

Living a life full of compassion leads to deep fulfillment. There's something inherently rewarding about helping others, especially when it is done selflessly. Compassion allows us to live in a way that transcends our own needs, focusing instead on the needs of others. It connects us to something larger than ourselves: a sense of shared humanity, the understanding that we are all together. Proverbs 11:25 says, *"A generous person will prosper; whoever refreshes others will be refreshed."* This reflects the truth that compassion doesn't just impact those we help—it also nourishes our soul. Offering care and kindness often leads to joy and personal growth. It deepens our empathy and broadens our understanding of the world.

How to Cultivate Compassion in Everyday Life
Listen actively: Compassion starts with listening. Ignoring others or dismissing their struggles in our busy lives is easy. But when we truly listen to someone's pain or joy, we understand their world and respond more meaningfully.

Step Out of Your Comfort Zone: Kindness frequently requires us to embrace awkwardness. Whether it's making a difference to somebody we do not know well or offering help in a situation that feels unbalanced, compassion asks us to step outside of our self-interest and focus on the needs of others.

Pray for Others: Prayer is an important way to cultivate compassion. It helps us see others through God's eyes, asking Him to help us have a heart full of mercy and grace for those suffering.

Give Your Time, Not Just Your Resources: While material help is valuable, sometimes the most compassionate thing we can offer is our time. Spending time with someone lonely or sick can be more impactful than a physical gift.

Look for Opportunities to Serve: Compassion is action. Look for ways to serve others in your community, whether volunteering at a local shelter, helping a neighbor, or simply being there for a needy friend.

Practice Empathy: Try to put yourself in others' shoes. Understanding someone else's pain or situation makes you more likely to feel moved to help.

The Significance of Feeding the Hungry

Feeding the hungry isn't a social obligation—it's a significant act of kindness, benevolence, and faith. The importance of nourishing the hungry lies in its capacity to address one of the most fundamental human needs, food. But it goes beyond that. It is an act that reflects the heart of God and illustrates His love for all people, particularly those who are most vulnerable.

Scriptural Foundation

In Matthew 25:35-40, Jesus makes a powerful statement about the importance of caring for those in need, saying, *"For I was hungry, and you gave me something to eat, I was thirsty, and you gave me something to drink, I was a stranger, and you welcomed me in, I needed clothes, and you clothed me..."* In this passage, Jesus identifies Himself with the hungry, the thirsty, the stranger, and the sick, urging His followers to serve these people as if they were serving Christ Himself.

This powerful passage teaches that feeding the hungry isn't simply about giving a meal—it's about recognizing the dignity of those in need, seeing them as valuable, and meeting their needs in a way that mirrors God's love for us. It directly reflects the commandment to love our neighbors as ourselves.

The Impact of Feeding the Hungry
Feeding the hungry is a means of meeting both physical and spiritual needs. Physically, it provides life-sustaining nourishment. For many who are homeless, jobless, or marginalized, hunger is a daily struggle. Providing food is not just about filling an empty stomach; it's about offering hope and restoring dignity. When someone receives a meal, it serves as a reminder that they are seen, cared for, and loved.

Spiritually, feeding the hungry is an expression of our faith in action. It reflects the kind of love God calls us to show—selfless, sacrificial, and unconditional. Jesus Himself often fed the hungry, whether through miracles like feeding the 5,000 in John 6:5–13 or providing meals for those who followed Him. By doing so, He demonstrated that meeting people's physical needs is integral to spreading the love and message of God's kingdom.

I remember volunteering at a food bank in a community hit hard by unemployment and poverty. The first day I served, the gratitude in people's eyes struck me, the relief in their voices, and the bonds formed as people connected over something as simple as a meal. It was a reminder that food has a deeper significance—it brings people together, restores dignity, and reminds people that they are not forgotten.

Feeding the Hungry as a Way of Living Purposefully

Feeding the hungry is more than an occasional act of kindness—it's a way of life for those who live purposefully. It reflects a life of intentionality and care for others. When we commit to feeding the hungry, we are embracing a mindset of generosity and selflessness that can transform not only the lives of others but also our own.

In 1 John 3:17-18, we read, *"If anyone has material possessions and sees a brother or sister in need but has no pity on them, how can the love of God be in that person? Dear children, let us not love with words or speech but with actions and in truth."* This passage challenges us to move beyond passive concern and into active service.

Living with purpose means that our actions align with our values. When we commit to feeding the hungry, we align ourselves with

God's heart—loving and caring for those in need. We embrace a life of empathy, recognizing that what we do for others reflects our faith and desire to make a meaningful difference.

Practical Ways to Feed the Hungry
Feeding the hungry doesn't always require grand gestures; even small acts of kindness can significantly impact.

Donate to Food Banks or Pantries
Many communities have local food banks where you can donate nonperishable items or funds to help provide meals to those in need.

Volunteer at Soup Kitchens or Shelters
Many cities have organizations that provide free meals to homeless individuals or low income families. Volunteering your time is a direct way to serve the hungry.

Support Meal Programs
Churches, schools, and community groups often offer meal programs that serve the homeless and low income families. Contributing to or supporting these programs ensures that individuals in need receive consistent meals.

Start a Community Food Drive
Organize food collection events at your local church or

community center to help stock food pantries or shelters.

Offer a Meal to a Neighbor in Need

Sometimes, the greatest needs are close to home. If you know someone struggling, offer to make a meal for them or invite them to share a meal with you.

The Heart of Feeding the Hungry

Feeding the hungry is not just about providing food—it's about creating an atmosphere of love, kindness, and belonging. It's about seeing the world through God's eyes, acknowledging the worth of every individual, and meeting their needs with a heart full of compassion.

Luke 6:38 says, *"Give, and it will be given to you. A good measure, pressed down, shaken together, and running over, will be poured into your lap. For with the measure you use, it will be measured to you."* This verse reminds us that giving, especially when it comes to feeding others, not only meets their needs but also enriches our lives. In feeding the hungry, we tap into a deeper well of generosity, compassion, and faith—living a life that reflects the love of Christ and the purpose He has for us.

The Significance of Generosity in Purposeful Living

Generosity is one of the most powerful forces that shape a purposeful life. It's not just about giving away money or possessions—generosity is a mindset. This lifestyle is deeply rooted in the idea of sharing what we have, no matter how much or how little, for the benefit of others. True generosity is about giving without expecting anything in return; in doing so, we align ourselves with God's heart.

Generosity in the Bible

Throughout Scripture, we see countless examples of generosity. Proverbs 11:25 says, *"A generous person will prosper; whoever refreshes others will be refreshed."* This is not merely a promise but a reflection of a deeper truth: generosity has a way of circling back to bless the giver. When we choose to be generous, it's as if we tap into a divine flow of blessings that nourish our hearts and lives.

The story of the widow's offering in Mark 12:41–44 is a profound example of what true generosity looks like. Jesus observes a poor widow who gives two small coins—her entire livelihood. While others give out of their wealth, the widow gives all she has. Jesus points to her and declares that she has given more than all the others because her gift came from a place of sacrifice and trust. Her generosity was not about the amount, but the heart behind it. Generosity is often counterintuitive in a world that values self-preservation and wealth accumulation. But biblical generosity is not limited to material wealth. It's about time, energy, attention, and love. In 2 Corinthians 9:7, Paul writes, *"Each of you should give what you have decided in your heart to give, not reluctantly or under compulsion, for God loves a cheerful giver."* The emphasis here is on the heart—the willingness to give freely, cheerfully, and generously.

Generosity Transforms Us

When we live generously, we break free from the chains of materialism and self-centeredness. Generosity teaches us that life is about relationships and connections, not just possessions. It reminds us that everything we have is a gift from God and that we are stewards, not owners, of our resources. The more we give, the more we realize that our wealth is not measured in what we accumulate but in how much we give away.

Generosity also has a deep impact on our personal growth. It nurtures a spirit of humility and compassion. The more we give, the more we open ourselves up to the needs of others. Generosity stretches our capacity for empathy and teaches us to see beyond ourselves.

I remember a time when I volunteered at a local shelter that helped families in crisis. I went there intending to serve, but I left feeling overwhelmingly blessed. The stories of those I met—parents struggling to provide for their children, individuals fighting battles with addiction, and families rebuilding their lives—taught me the true meaning of generosity. It wasn't just about giving what I had; it was about sharing in their struggle, showing up for them, and offering whatever I could, whether food, time, or a listening ear. That experience transformed my perspective on generosity, making me realize that it isn't just about material things—it's about showing up for others in ways that cost us something, even if it's just our time and attention.

Jesus regularly spoke about charity and selflessness in the Kingdom of God. In Matthew 25:35-40, Jesus says, *"For I was hungry and you gave me something to eat, I was thirsty, and you gave me something to drink, I was a stranger and you invited me in..."* This verse emphasizes that assisting others, especially those in need, is one of the clearest ways to reflect the ideals of God's Kingdom. When we contribute to others, we are serving Christ Himself.

In this sense, generosity isn't just about handing out charity; it's about recognizing the humanity and dignity of others and responding with compassion. Jesus challenges us to see the world through His eyes and to treat the hungry, the thirsty, and the stranger as if they were Christ Himself.

Generosity as a Pathway to Purpose
Living a purposeful life means living with a sense of mission; generosity is one key where we fulfill that mission. It might be easy to think that purpose is found in great accomplishments or

personal success, but our purpose is deeply connected to how we serve and bless others. We participate in God's greater purpose for the world every time we give—whether through our finances, time, or talents.

Generosity doesn't have to be grand or spectacular. It can be found in everyday moments: paying for a stranger's coffee, offering your seat to someone in need, helping a neighbor with groceries, or simply taking time to listen to someone who feels unheard. These small acts of generosity can create ripples of impact far beyond what we can see.

Actionable Steps on How to Live Generously

Give without expectations: Generosity is not about getting something in return. Give from the heart without thinking about how you'll benefit.

Be intentional with your time

Sometimes, the most generous gift we can offer is our time. Whether volunteering, helping a friend, or just listening to someone who needs to talk, giving your time can make a huge difference in someone's life.

Practice regular acts of kindness

Start small buy someone a meal, help a neighbor with chores, or donate to a cause you care about. These actions create a habit of generosity that becomes a natural part of your life.

Serve joyfully

Look for ways to serve in your community, church, or workplace. Serving others, small or large, helps you live out your purpose and positively impact the world.

Support those in need

Look for opportunities to help those struggling, whether offering financial help, donating clothes, or giving food to a food bank. Your generosity doesn't always need to be grand but should always be heartfelt.

The Significance of Loving in Purposeful Living

Love is the most powerful force in the universe—the thread that binds us together, the fuel that drives our actions, and the essence of what makes life meaningful. The Bible teaches us that love is not just an emotion but a choice—a way of living. In 1 Corinthians 13:4–7, Paul describes love as patient, kind, and unselfish—qualities that reflect the heart of God and should be reflected in our relationships with others.

Love as The Foundation of Purpose

Without love, all our actions become empty, no matter how noble. In 1 Corinthians 13:1–3, Paul writes, *"If I speak in the tongues of men or angels, but do not have love, I am only a resounding gong or a clanging cymbal. If I have the gift of prophecy and can fathom all mysteries and all knowledge, and if I have a faith that can move mountains but do not have love, I am nothing."* This passage is a powerful reminder that love is not a mere accessory to purposeful living, but the foundation upon which everything else is built.

When we live with love at the center of our lives, we see the world differently. We recognize that every person is created in God's image and worthy of respect, dignity, and care. Love transforms how we interact with others—from how we treat strangers to how we cherish our closest relationships.

Love in Action: Demonstrating God's Love to the World

The ultimate example of love in action is in John 3:16, which says, *"For God so loved the world that He gave His one and only Son, that whoever believes in Him shall not perish but have eternal life."* God's love is sacrificial, unconditional, and selfless. Through the life, death, and resurrection of Jesus Christ, God demonstrated the greatest act of love possible. This love calls us to a higher standard, where we love others even when it's difficult, inconvenient, or costly.

One of the most powerful ways we can live with purpose is by showing this same sacrificial love to those around us. This doesn't always mean grand gestures or heroic actions—it's often the small, daily choices to act with kindness, patience, and understanding. Whether it's offering a listening ear to a friend in need, helping a neighbor with a difficult task, or standing up for someone being mistreated, love compels us to care for the well-being of others, even when it's not easy.

I once had a colleague going through a difficult season in her personal life. She often seemed distant and withdrawn, and I could sense she was carrying a heavy burden. One day, I decided to reach out—not to fix her problems, but to offer my presence. I invited her to lunch and listened as she shared her struggles. At that moment, she didn't need advice or solutions—she just needed someone who would listen and care. Love is sometimes as simple as showing up for others and letting them know they are not alone.

The Challenge of Love
While loving those close to us is often natural, Jesus calls us to a love that extends even to our enemies. In Matthew 5:44, Jesus commands, *"But I tell you, love your enemies and pray for those who persecute you."* This is a challenging and radical form of love that defies human nature. It is easy to love those who love us in return, but true love reaches beyond that.

This kind of love requires humility, patience, and the willingness to forgive. It asks us to lay down our pride, to choose reconciliation over division, and to seek peace even when it seems impossible. Loving our enemies doesn't mean we condone harmful actions, but we choose not to repay evil with evil. Instead, we trust God to handle justice while we focus on offering grace, understanding, and forgiveness.

I remember having a strained relationship with someone in my life due to a misunderstanding. The bitterness and hurt were deep, and for a long time, I struggled to forgive. However, I felt compelled to try—not for the sake of the other person but for mine. I prayed for strength and began to soften my heart. Over time, I rebuilt trust and restored that relationship—not because the person deserved it, but because I understood that love is the most powerful way to heal wounds.

The Call to Love in Our Daily Lives

So, how do we put love into action in our everyday lives? Here are a few practical steps:

Start with Self Love

Before truly loving others, we must learn to love ourselves. This doesn't mean being self-centered but recognizing our worth in God's eyes. As Matthew 22:39 says, *"Love your neighbor as yourself."* Self-love means treating ourselves with kindness, respecting our needs, and nurturing our spiritual, emotional, and physical well-being.

Practice Patience and Kindness

We encounter opportunities to be patient and kind daily. Whether waiting in a long line at the grocery store or dealing with someone rude or difficult, love gives us the strength to respond with grace instead of frustration.

Forgive and Let Go

Forgiveness is an act of love. When we forgive others, we free ourselves from the burden of bitterness. It doesn't always mean forgetting, but it means choosing not to hold grudges. Forgiveness is a gift we give both to others and ourselves.

Serve with a Loving Heart

True love is seen in action. Whether helping a friend, volunteering in your community, or serving your family, showing love through your actions will often speak louder than words.

Extend Love to Strangers

Often, the most profound ways to demonstrate love are with those we don't know. Showing kindness to a stranger a smile, a small act of service, a word of encouragement can make a world of difference. You never know what someone is going through, but your simple gesture could remind them of God's love for them.

Love is the Answer

Love is what gives our lives meaning. 1 John 4:7 8 says, *"Dear friends, let us love one another, for love comes from God. Everyone who loves has been born of God and knows God. Whoever does not love does not know God because God is love."* Love is not merely a feeling; it is the very essence of who God is. And as we love, we reflect His character to the world.

Purposeful living is not about achieving personal goals or finding success at the expense of others it is about living out love. When we love deeply, we live purposefully, reflecting God's love for us.

The Significance of Serving Others

Service is one of the most impactful ways to live a purposeful life, aligning directly with the heart of Christ's ministry. In Matthew 20:28, Jesus Himself tells us, *"The Son of Man did not come to be served, but to serve, and to give His life as a ransom for many."* This powerful verse illustrates the essence of service: it's not about our glory but about humbling ourselves and meeting the needs of others.

Serving others is about being the hands and feet of Christ in the world, using our time, talents, and resources to help those in need. Service can be big and small—sometimes, it's a grand, life-changing act, and other times, it's a simple, everyday kindness.

But in all things, serving others requires a heart of humility and selflessness.

The Call to Serve: What Does It Mean?

Serving others is more than just fulfilling an obligation—it's a lifestyle. It's about intentionally looking for opportunities to make the lives of others better without expecting anything in return. Service is not just about what we can do for others but also about how we position ourselves to make a positive difference in the lives of those around us.

In Mark 9:35, Jesus teaches us about greatness in the kingdom of God: *"Anyone who wants to be first must be the very last, and the servant of all."* True greatness is not measured by power, wealth, or prestige but by how well we serve others. Jesus flipped the conventional idea of greatness on its head, showing that the most valuable people in God's kingdom are those who choose to serve. Think about how powerful that perspective can be in our daily lives. How can we improve our workplaces, families, and communities? It begins with service. Whether we help a coworker with a project, offer a kind word to a stranger, or volunteer at a local charity, each act of service contributes to a greater purpose.

The Transformational Power of Service

Serving others can transform both the giver and the receiver. I remember being part of a mission trip that involved going to a small village to help build homes for impoverished families. The project was physically demanding—long days of manual labor in intense heat—but the moment we handed over the keys to the new homes, the look of joy and relief on the faces of those families was indescribable. In that moment, I realized that service doesn't just meet physical needs; it restores dignity and hope.

Similarly, serving others can heal our hearts. Acts of service put us in a posture of humility, allowing us to step outside of our struggles and focus on the needs of others. In doing so, we find purpose and fulfillment. It's a beautiful paradox: the more we give, the more we receive. Jesus promised in Luke 6:38, *"Give, and it will be given to you. A good measure, pressed down, shaken together, and running over, will be poured into your lap"*.

Practical Ways to Serve Others

Service doesn't always need to be a large-scale mission trip or charity event. There are countless ways we can serve those around us every day:

In Our Families

Serving starts at home. Whether helping with household chores, offering support to a spouse, or spending quality time with our children, our families are the first place where service should be demonstrated. These small, everyday acts of service build a foundation for a life of purpose.

In Our Communities

Volunteering at a local food bank, helping clean up a park, or offering your time to a community event there are always opportunities to serve in our neighborhoods. The impact of these acts is often far reaching, as they foster a sense of community and belonging.

In the Workplace

Serving can even take place in our professional lives. Helping a colleague with a project, offering encouragement to a struggling coworker, or making the workplace more positive by being kind and thoughtful these actions help create a supportive environment.

Through Financial or Material Giving

For some, serving might look like donating to a cause, offering financial support to someone in need, or donating unused items to those who can benefit from them. The key is to be willing to give what we have, whether time, resources, or energy.

The Benefits of Serving Others

Devoting oneself to the service of others brings a deeper sense of fulfillment to life. Acts 20:35 beautifully conveys the sentiment that giving is a greater joy than receiving. In serving, our spirits are nurtured, our emotions deepen, and our connections with others flourish. Engaging in service allows us to nurture a deep sense of compassion, humility, and empathy—vital qualities for a life filled with meaning and intention.

It also strengthens our connection with God. Colossians 3:23-24 teaches us that *"whatever you do, work at it with all your heart, as working for the Lord, not for human masters, since you know that you will receive an inheritance from the Lord as a reward."* This means that no act of service is unnoticed by God, no matter how small. Every time we serve others, we are serving Him.

Serving others also brings us closer to Christ's heart. Jesus did not come to be served but to serve, and by following His example, we align our hearts with His. In this way, service becomes a form of worship.

Actionable Steps to Serve Others
Identify the Needs Around You: Take some time to observe your environment at home, work, or in your community and see where there are needs. Often, the needs are clear if we take a moment to stop and look.

Make Time for Service: Service requires time and energy, so it's important to prioritize it. Set aside time each week or month to volunteer, help a neighbor, or support someone in need.

Practice Selfless Giving: Look for ways to give without expecting anything in return. It could be financial, material, or simply giving your time and attention.

Serve with a Willing Heart: Always approach service with joy, not obligation. Remember that in serving others, you are ultimately serving God.

IMPACT AND 8 CONTRIBUTION

Impact and Contribution. Throughout my life, I have made it my mission to serve others and positively impact the communities I am a part of. From my humble beginnings in Kenya to my career in healthcare in the U.S., I have continually been guided by a deep sense of purpose and a desire to help others. My contributions span several areas: education, healthcare, mission work, and community service.

...I learned the power of leading by example and realized that even small actions could inspire significant change.

Community Engagement and Education in Kenya

Growing up in Kenya, I learned early on the importance of sharing and caring for those in need. My parents instilled compassion, responsibility, and generosity in me. As a child, I was actively involved in community service, often accompanying my mother to deliver food to widows and orphans. I learned to share with others, recognizing the importance of lifting those who were struggling.

In our village, I also actively participated in teaching the children in my church. I conducted music lessons, led prayer meetings, and even imitated the adults during the youth week of prayer. My efforts to engage and inspire the younger generation of my community helped many find their faith, and several individuals were baptized due to our activities. Through these experiences, I learned the power of leading by example and realized that even small actions could inspire significant change.

Founding Maurice Ojwang Unique Academy

As I moved forward, I continued to stay connected to my roots and the desire to give back to the community. My husband and I co-founded Maurice Ojwang Unique Academy, an institution dedicated to providing quality education to children who otherwise would not have access to it. This school has allowed countless children to learn, grow, and pursue their dreams, regardless of their financial background.

Through our work with the academy, we have provided education and supported needy families by offering scholarships and financial assistance. This has allowed children from underprivileged backgrounds to attend school, breaking the cycle of poverty and paving the way for a brighter future.

Mission Work and Health Fairs

In addition to my work in leadership, I have contributed to my community through mission work. In 1998, I led a mission trip to Kenya with 30 people from our local Church. While there, we organized health fairs, clothing drives, and counseling services for the local population. We contacted over 500 individuals, offering them support, guidance, and essential healthcare services. This mission work impacted the lives of those we helped and inspired a lasting connection between the church in the U.S. and the Kenyan community.

Healthcare Leaders and Service in the U.S.

Upon relocating to the United States, I transitioned into a healthcare career, initially working as a nursing assistant before becoming a Licensed Practical Nurse (LPN), and then a Registered Nurse (RN). I continued to pursue education, earning a Bachelor's in Nursing and a Master's in Nursing with an emphasis in leadership.

I have significantly contributed to patient care, leadership, and staff development throughout my healthcare career. As a nurse manager, I have overseen my unit's daily operations and mentored and developed healthcare professionals, fostering an environment of collaboration, compassion, and excellence. My commitment to improving patient care and supporting my team has earned me respect.

Personal and Professional Resilience

The passing of my husband due to COVID-19 in 2020 was a pivotal moment in my life, one that forced me to re-evaluate my purpose and my contributions to the world. Despite the immense personal loss, I chose to continue pursuing my purpose of service, focusing on my children and their education. I relocated to be closer to my family and continued to work in healthcare leadership while reflecting on my purpose and commitment to helping others.

Core Values and Legacy

A deep sense of purpose has shaped my life's journey. My purpose is to serve others—through educating children, providing healthcare, or leading by example in my community. My contributions, from founding a school in Kenya to working in healthcare leadership in the U.S., are driven by a desire to improve the world for future generations.

As I reflect on my life's work, I am proud of my impact on the lives of those I have served. My legacy is one of compassion, service, and leadership, and I am committed to continuing this work for as long as possible.

CONCLUSION

As I reflect on the journey I've shared in this book, I hope you feel inspired to live with greater intention and purpose. Purposeful living isn't always easy, but it's always worth it. It's about understanding your values, facing challenges with courage, and embracing every opportunity to grow, serve, and give. It's about finding ways—even in the smallest actions—to make a difference in the lives of others.

I've seen firsthand how choosing to live with purpose can transform our lives and the lives of those around us. It doesn't matter where you start, but the direction you choose. By cultivating kindness, generosity, and compassion, we enrich our journeys and help light the way for others.

As you continue to live out your purpose, I hope you remember that each step is a chance to make a positive impact. We can all shape the world meaningfully, starting with small, purposeful daily actions.

Purposeful living isn't about perfection. It's about intention, faith, and the willingness to keep going, no matter the obstacles. I encourage you to step forward, trust your values and calling, and live with purpose that will echo beyond your life.

INDEX

A

abilities, 13, 15, 26, 37, 45, 46, 75, 77, 80, 87, 88, 141
adolescence, 4
adulthood, 3, 25
adults, 3, 200

B

beliefs, 14, 50, 61, 62, 63, 65, 83, 98, 102, 104, 105, 125, 140
believe, 3, 6, 42, 50, 56, 72, 76, 81, 82, 125, 137, 176
Bible, 20, 21, 98, 102, 116, 117, 127, 128, 129, 139, 144, 147, 153, 158, 160, 166, 167, 170, 176, 184, 189

C

calling, 4, 9, 50, 60, 71, 72, 77, 125, 144, 147, 150, 160, 167
caring, 5, 12, 19, 34, 43, 92, 94, 145, 179, 182, 200
challenges, 4, 9, 17, 21, 23, 24, 43, 44, 45, 47, 55, 71, 74, 75, 82, 95, 97, 106, 108, 111, 114, 124, 135, 182, 187, 204
children's, 2, 7, 20, 25
Christians, 82, 147
church, 2, 3, 4, 5, 6, 8, 9, 20, 21, 23, 25, 147, 149, 168, 183, 189, 200, 202
commitment, 1, 4, 5, 9, 12, 15, 25, 38, 47, 67, 70, 73, 82, 95, 99, 105, 113, 124, 126, 136, 158, 161, 162, 202, 203
community, 1, 2, 3, 4, 5, 7, 8, 14, 15, 17, 19, 20, 21, 23, 24, 25, 26, 28, 31, 42, 43, 54, 80, 91, 102, 120, 123, 124, 126, 140, 144, 145, 156, 163, 168, 169, 173, 175, 178, 181, 182, 183, 189, 193, 197, 199, 200, 201, 203
community service, 1
crises, 10, 11, 13, 18

D

debt, 90
decisions, 30, 34, 43, 44, 65, 66, 72, 92, 118
difference, 3, 9, 15, 46, 47, 51, 58, 68, 72, 75, 87, 88, 89, 93, 103, 120, 126, 130, 135, 148, 156, 161, 168, 169, 175, 178, 182, 188, 193, 195, 204
dreams, 67, 68, 69, 71, 78, 201

E

educating, 12, 203

education, 3, 4, 7, 21, 23, 24, 25, 26, 28, 29, 30, 31, 32, 34, 36, 37, 38, 39, 40, 41, 47, 57, 71, 200, 201, 202, 203
environment, 27, 37, 42, 43, 47, 82, 91, 93, 94, 97, 100, 120, 123, 197, 199, 202
experience, 3, 8, 14, 15, 25, 27, 31, 32, 33, 35, 45, 46, 47, 54, 63, 68, 74, 78, 106, 107, 110, 111, 113, 126, 130, 136, 139, 171, 176, 186
experiences, 1, 2, 9, 14, 20, 21, 25, 49, 55, 61, 62, 64, 70, 71, 74, 80, 95, 112, 140, 142, 201

F

faith, 3, 4, 9, 20, 23, 25, 70, 102, 103, 104, 105, 110, 115, 116, 118, 119, 125, 128, 129, 133, 144, 145, 146, 147, 150, 151, 164, 166, 167, 180, 182, 184, 190, 201
family, 1, 5, 6, 19, 20, 21, 23, 24, 25, 38, 57, 64, 65, 70, 73, 87, 92, 98, 103, 104, 105, 169, 172, 175, 193, 203
feelings, 54, 64, 97, 99, 123, 149
finances, 24, 25, 90, 91, 188
food, 2, 20, 24, 70, 93, 136, 156, 168, 179, 180, 181, 182, 183, 186, 189, 197, 200
forgiveness, 98, 171, 172, 192
foundation, 7, 25, 44, 46, 70, 71, 72, 76, 92, 102, 104, 112, 115, 127, 138, 159, 170, 190, 197

G

game, 70
gift, 2, 71, 82, 88, 136, 145, 168, 176, 178, 185, 188, 189, 193
girl, 2
give, 2, 6, 20, 26, 27, 30, 33, 34, 35, 38, 51, 57, 61, 65, 71, 75, 77, 78, 89, 90, 91, 105, 110, 114, 123, 127, 128, 129, 130, 131, 132, 133, 135, 136, 144, 156, 162, 170, 172, 185, 186, 188, 193, 194, 196, 198, 199, 201, 204
goal, 42, 44, 45, 48, 51, 52, 68, 69, 95, 124, 159, 160, 172
goals, 16, 27, 49, 52, 53, 61, 66, 67, 68, 69, 73, 78, 79, 80, 82, 83, 84, 87, 91, 92, 113, 115, 120, 123, 124, 126, 162, 194
God, 8, 58, 82, 98, 99, 101, 102, 106, 116, 117, 118, 119, 122, 128, 129, 131, 132, 133, 134, 136, 137, 138, 139, 140, 141, 142, 143, 144, 146, 147, 148, 149, 150, 151, 153, 154, 159, 160, 163, 164, 165, 166, 167, 169, 170, 171, 172, 173, 176, 178, 179, 180, 181, 182, 183, 184, 185, 186, 187, 189, 190, 192, 194, 195, 198, 199

H

happiness, 49, 109, 127, 131
happy, 22, 64, 78
health, 5, 10, 11, 12, 13, 15, 16, 17, 18, 30, 31, 32, 33, 34, 42, 45, 46, 47, 49, 54, 59, 62, 67, 109, 175, 202
healthcare, 5, 8, 9, 10, 11, 12, 14, 15, 16, 17, 18, 25, 26, 27, 28, 29, 31, 32, 33, 35, 36, 37, 38, 39, 40, 41, 42, 43, 44, 45, 46, 47, 71, 124, 200, 202, 203
household, 1, 20, 85, 86, 197
humanitarian, 1, 7, 9, 10, 11, 12, 13, 15, 16, 17, 18, 25, 45, 47
humanitarian services, 1

I

identity, 137, 138, 139, 140, 141, 142
individuals, 1, 3, 4, 7, 13, 14, 17, 98, 125, 140, 144, 160, 168, 179, 182, 183, 186, 201, 202
influence, 2, 19, 21, 46, 95, 103, 104, 105, 106, 110, 115, 117
issues, 10, 17, 27, 36, 47, 100, 111, 116, 175

J

Jesus, 22, 98, 103, 117, 118, 122, 128, 130, 133, 137, 140, 141, 160, 166, 167, 170, 171, 175, 177, 179, 180, 184, 186, 187, 190, 191, 194, 195, 196, 198

K

Kenya, 1, 3, 4, 5, 7, 19, 26, 200, 202, 203
kindness, 2, 20, 64, 73, 95, 101, 102, 103, 104, 105, 106, 108, 110, 116, 119, 121, 122, 126, 129, 134, 135, 136, 137, 147, 153, 154, 155, 156, 157, 163, 164, 165, 167, 169, 173, 174, 176, 177, 179, 181, 182, 183, 188, 191, 193, 195, 204
knowledge, 15, 26, 29, 30, 31, 35, 38, 39, 41, 45, 46, 54, 55, 77, 91, 95, 124, 139, 189

L

leader, 2, 4, 42, 47, 71, 88
leadership, 2, 5, 14, 23, 26, 28, 29, 35, 36, 42, 43, 44, 45, 46, 47, 71, 202, 203
learning, 21, 25, 37, 38, 39, 74, 108, 111, 113, 114, 124, 163, 170
lessons, 1, 2, 24, 25, 46, 70, 71, 74, 78, 106, 112, 126, 200
life, 1, 4, 8, 9, 11, 12, 15, 19, 20, 21, 22, 23, 24, 25, 27, 34, 37, 44, 48, 49, 50, 51, 52, 53, 54, 55, 56, 57, 58, 59, 60, 61, 62, 63, 66, 67, 70, 71, 72, 74, 75, 76, 77, 78, 79, 80, 81, 82, 83, 84, 92, 94, 96, 102, 103, 105, 106, 107, 109, 110, 111, 112, 113, 114, 115, 116, 117, 119, 120, 122, 123, 126, 127, 129, 130, 131, 132, 133, 134, 135, 136, 138, 141, 143, 144, 145, 146, 147, 148, 150, 151, 154, 157, 160, 162, 168, 169, 170, 172, 173, 174, 177, 180, 181, 182, 184, 185, 187, 188, 189, 190, 191, 192, 194, 195, 197, 198, 200, 203
lifestyle, 3, 61, 68, 85, 150, 184, 195
lives, 1, 2, 3, 9, 11, 15, 17, 20, 21, 26, 43, 45, 53, 72, 75, 77, 78, 80, 89, 90, 93, 95, 96, 98, 101, 103, 107, 109, 111, 113, 118, 119, 120, 121, 123, 125, 126, 128, 129, 131, 133, 134, 136, 138, 144, 148, 149, 150, 151, 153, 160, 162, 167, 169, 170, 171, 174, 175, 178, 181, 183, 184, 186, 190, 192, 194, 195, 196, 197, 202, 203, 204
love, 19, 20, 23, 26, 58, 77, 78, 81, 99, 100, 101, 111, 116, 117, 118, 119, 121, 122, 128, 129, 130, 131, 132, 133, 134, 135, 136, 138, 140, 141, 142, 143, 144, 145, 146, 149, 150, 151, 153, 154, 155, 167, 171, 172, 173, 174, 180, 181, 183, 184, 185, 189, 190, 191, 192, 193, 194

M

medical, 5, 6, 10, 12, 13, 16, 18, 26, 27, 35, 38, 39, 45, 46, 47
mentor, 4, 105, 156
mindful, 91, 92, 105
ministry, 2, 177, 194

mission, 1, 7, 16, 44, 77, 119, 127, 151, 187, 196, 197, 200, 201
missionary, 5
moral, 122, 125, 166
mother, 1, 2, 19, 20, 25, 70, 72, 200

N

Nairobi, 19, 22, 23
nursing, 1, 4, 5, 6, 10, 12, 14, 15, 16, 26, 27, 28, 29, 30, 31, 32, 33, 34, 35, 36, 37, 38, 39, 40, 41, 45, 47, 71, 202

O

obligations, 7, 38, 152
obstacles, 30, 38, 79, 81, 111, 112, 114, 115, 116, 123, 141, 160
orphans, 2, 20, 200
outreach programs, 5

P

person, 1, 48, 54, 55, 57, 60, 62, 65, 72, 73, 74, 76, 77, 83, 86, 93, 95, 99, 125, 127, 129, 130, 143, 145, 155, 167, 177, 181, 184, 190, 192
populations, 10, 11, 18, 35, 45, 46
power, 2, 3, 9, 17, 56, 88, 106, 112, 117, 148, 176, 195, 201
practice, 2, 17, 27, 28, 29, 30, 31, 32, 34, 37, 39, 41, 50, 62, 66, 69, 107, 129, 144, 162, 165
pray, 3, 101, 140, 172, 191
prayer, 3, 71, 117, 140, 149, 170, 200
preachers, 3, 22
principle, 82, 99, 127, 162, 165
production, 93, 94
progression, 28
purpose, 1, 4, 8, 9, 15, 20, 24, 25, 48, 49, 50, 51, 52, 53, 54, 55, 56, 57, 58, 59, 60, 70, 71, 72, 75, 76, 77, 80, 82, 88, 89, 90, 102, 105, 106, 110, 111, 112, 115, 116, 117, 118, 119, 120, 122, 123, 124, 125, 126, 127, 129, 130, 131, 132, 133, 134, 136, 137, 139, 141, 142, 143, 144, 150, 151, 154, 158, 159, 160, 165, 170, 171, 172, 173, 175, 182, 184, 187, 189, 190, 196, 197, 200, 203, 204

R

relationships, 64, 73, 98, 99, 101, 103, 108, 109, 117, 118, 121, 124, 126, 130, 144, 159, 162, 169, 171, 172, 173, 185, 189, 190
resilience, 1, 4, 9, 14, 17, 24, 25, 65, 70, 74, 75, 82, 95, 97, 105, 106, 107, 108, 109, 110, 111, 112, 115, 116, 121, 123, 139, 145
responsibility, 3, 9, 19, 21, 24, 25, 34, 41, 42, 56, 70, 72, 92, 93, 98, 144, 165, 174, 200
roles, 5, 29, 34, 35, 41, 46, 71, 72, 77

S

selflessness, 1, 121, 128, 134, 135, 141, 181, 186, 195
service, 1, 3, 4, 5, 8, 9, 22, 25, 49, 64, 75, 80, 81, 102, 103, 104, 105, 110, 117, 120, 122, 126, 136, 140, 161, 174, 182, 193, 194, 196, 197, 198, 199, 200, 203
serving, 4, 15, 20, 54, 71, 103, 117, 119, 122, 135, 163, 180, 187, 193, 195, 196, 197, 198, 199
Seventh-day Adventist, 1, 2, 3, 20, 23
skills, 2, 5, 9, 11, 17, 27, 28, 29, 31, 32, 35, 36, 37, 40, 46, 56, 69, 74, 76, 77, 88, 91, 95, 113, 114, 124, 128, 132, 135, 157
song, 2
steward, 88, 89, 90, 132
strangers, 163, 164, 165, 166, 167, 168, 190
strength, 8, 55, 71, 74, 79, 99, 102, 106, 108, 111, 116, 140, 142, 144, 145, 146, 149, 192, 193
success, 9, 25, 42, 63, 68, 75, 89, 116, 141, 150, 161, 163, 187, 194

T

task, 69, 70, 72, 87, 95, 191
teaching, 2, 12, 15, 20, 30, 39, 46, 70, 112, 114, 128, 135, 167, 200
time, 4, 5, 8, 19, 20, 21, 22, 23, 32, 38, 43, 51, 53, 55, 56, 63, 64, 67, 68, 70, 74, 75, 82, 83, 84, 85, 86, 87, 90, 91, 96, 102, 104, 105, 112, 114, 123, 124, 128, 132, 135, 136, 148, 149, 158, 162, 168, 169, 171, 172, 175, 178, 182, 185, 186, 188, 192, 195, 197, 198, 199
titles, 72

U

U.S, 4, 8, 28, 200, 202, 203
United States, 1, 4, 8, 40, 41, 202
unity, 3

V

valuable, 24, 25, 74, 83, 89, 91, 114, 127, 133, 178, 195
values, 2, 4, 12, 14, 19, 23, 25, 40, 55, 56, 60, 61, 62, 63, 64, 65, 66, 67, 69, 72, 73, 74, 75, 83, 89, 92, 95, 98, 102, 104, 105, 106, 116, 119, 123, 125, 126, 129, 135, 136, 138, 142, 162, 174, 182, 185, 204
voluntary, 1, 3, 5

W

want, 49, 51, 52, 53, 56, 58, 65, 67, 68, 69, 79, 85, 86, 102, 104, 162
widows, 2, 20, 200
woman, 3

Y

youth, 4, 70, 200

GLOSSARY

Anhedonia – A condition where a person loses interest in activities that once brought joy, often linked to depression.

Anxious – A feeling of unease, worry, or nervousness, typically about an uncertain outcome.

Authority – The power or right to make decisions, give orders, or enforce rules, particularly in leadership and healthcare settings.

Autonomy – The ability to make independent decisions, often referring to patients' rights in healthcare.

Autonomy in Healthcare – The right of patients to make informed decisions about their medical treatment and care.

Baptism – A religious rite symbolizing purification, commitment, and acceptance into the faith.

Certifications – Official documents proving a person has met certain professional or educational standards.

Charity – The act of giving help to those in need, typically in the form of money, resources, or services.

Choir – A group of singers performing together, often in a religious or community setting.

Clinical – Relating to medical practice, patient care, or hospital environments.

Community – A group of people living together or sharing common interests, often involved in collective initiatives.

Community Health – A healthcare field focused on improving populations' health and well-being through education, prevention, and outreach programs.

Compassion – A deep awareness of and concern for the suffering of others, often leading to a desire to help.

Conflicts – Disagreements or struggles, whether personal, social, or global, that require resolution.

Consistent – Acting or performing reliably and steadily.

COVID-19 – A viral disease caused by the SARS-CoV-2 virus, leading to a global pandemic and significant health challenges.

Critical – Involving urgent or essential decision-making, often in life-threatening medical situations.

Criticism – The analysis, judgment, or evaluation of something, whether constructive or negative.

Curiosity – A strong desire to learn or understand something.

Desire – A deep longing or ambition to achieve something.

Diagnosing – Identifying a disease or condition through examination and medical tests.

Disparities – Differences or inequalities, often referring to access to healthcare and social resources.

Educators – Individuals who teach, train, or provide guidance formally or informally.

Emotional – Relating to a person's feelings and psychological well-being.

Empathy – The ability to understand and share the feelings of another.

Faith – Strong belief or trust, often in religious or spiritual matters.

Firm – Having a strong foundation, whether in belief, decision-making, or physical stability.

Fortitude – Strength and endurance when facing adversity.

Fragility – Being delicate or vulnerable, often applied to life situations or emotional conditions.

Future – The time ahead, encompassing plans, aspirations, and uncertainties.

God – A central religious belief figure representing divine authority and guidance.

Grievance – A complaint or concern arising from a perceived injustice or unfair treatment.

Habits – Repeated behaviors or routines that shape one's daily life.

Hardship – Severe suffering or difficulty, often due to economic, health, or personal struggles.

Highlight – To emphasize or bring attention to something important.

Holistic – Considering the whole person or system rather than just focusing on individual parts.

Humility – A modest view of one's importance, often paired with a willingness to learn and serve.

Identity – A person's sense of self, shaped by experiences, culture, and beliefs.

In re – A legal term meaning "in the matter of" or "regarding."

Independence – The ability to function or make decisions without reliance on others.

Influence – The power to affect others' behavior, opinions, or actions.

Initiatives – Programs or efforts undertaken to achieve a specific goal.

Livestock – Farm animals raised for food, labor, or agricultural purposes.

Mortgage – A financial agreement where property is used as security for a loan.

Mutual – Shared between two or more people, often referring to respect, understanding, or goals.

Natural Disasters – Catastrophic events such as earthquakes, hurricanes, and floods that cause widespread damage.

Nurse – A healthcare professional trained to care for patients, provide medical assistance, and promote wellness.

Obligations – Duties or commitments that a person is responsible for fulfilling.

Obstacles – Challenges or barriers that hinder progress.

Pediatrics – A branch of medicine focused on the health and care of infants, children, and adolescents.

Perseverance – The ability to persist through difficulties without giving up.

Practitioners – Professionals who apply their skills in a particular field, such as medicine or law.

Prioritize – To arrange tasks or responsibilities in order of importance.

Priority – Something that is regarded as more important than others.

Protracted – Extended or prolonged in time, often referring to conflicts or struggles.

Purpose – A sense of direction or meaning in life, often linked to personal values and goals.

Refugee – A person forced to flee their home due to war, persecution, or disaster.

Reputation – The beliefs or opinions generally held about someone or something.

Resilience – The ability to recover quickly from difficulties; mental or emotional strength.

Sabbath – A day of religious observance and rest, typically observed weekly.

Selflessness – Putting the needs of others before one's own without expecting anything in return.

Simultaneously – Occurring at the same time.

Spiritual – Relating to deep religious or personal beliefs.

Spur – To encourage or stimulate action.

Talents – Natural abilities or skills.

Testament – Evidence or proof of something, often linked to faith or legacy.

Therapy – Treatment designed to heal or alleviate medical or emotional issues.

Tradition – Practices, beliefs, or customs passed down through generations.

Triaging – The process of determining patients' priority based on their condition's severity.

Vigorous – Strong, active, and full of energy.

Vision – A long-term plan or goal for the future.

Voluntary – Done by choice rather than obligation, often referring to service work.

ABOUT THE AUTHOR

Dr. Linet Ojwang is a MD graduate with a nursing background. Her journey through healthcare, personal healing, and spiritual growth has made her a strong voice for living a life with purpose.

With a heart full of compassion and deep faith, she combines her medical knowledge with spiritual wisdom to help others. She is also the CEO of CareBridge Talent LLC.

Her book "The Essence and Importance of Living a Purposeful Life" is based on her life experiences, which were full of challenges, reflection, and growth. In it, she encourages readers to find their true identity and live with meaning, using honest stories and lessons from the Bible.

Dr. Ojwang also created Lin Purpose for Life, a YouTube channel and an upcoming podcast. There, she shares insight into health, purpose, and faith messages to inspire people to follow their calling and live with courage.

Whether caring for patients, writing, or speaking online, Dr. Linet Ojwang is committed to helping others live a life filled with hope, purpose, and spiritual strength.

www.ingramcontent.com/pod-product-compliance
Lightning Source LLC
Chambersburg PA
CBHW060951230426
43665CB00015B/2154